Bully-Proof Kids

Practical tools to help your child grow up
confident, resilient and strong

Stella O'Malley

Gill Books

Gill Books
Hume Avenue
Park West
Dublin 12
www.gillbooks.ie

Gill Books is an imprint of M.H. Gill & Co.

978 07171 7542 0

Designed by Síofra Murphy
Edited by Sheila Armstrong
Printed by Clays Limited, Suffolk

This book is typeset in TheSerif Light 11/17 pt

The paper used in this book comes from the wood pulp of managed forests. For every tree felled, at least one tree is planted, thereby renewing natural resources.

A CIP catalogue record for this book is available from the British Library.

5 4 3 2

Acknowledgements

I am often perplexed and unsure how to react when my friends and family assume that my work as a psychotherapist is draining or debilitating in some way. In fact, it's quite the opposite. My work has so far always been energy-giving and inspiring as the clients I work with are sensitive and generous enough to seek help and then willing to face the obstacles that invariably appear along the way. This book wouldn't have happened if not for the clients that I have been lucky enough to meet and I'd like to take this opportunity to give them my heartfelt thanks.

The book wouldn't have crossed over the line without the discernment and engagement of Sarah Liddy, so thanks for that. I'm also thankful to Sheila Armstrong, Teresa Daly and to everyone at Gill Books for their clear-minded judgement calls.

To my lovely Henry and darling kids, Róisín and Muiris, thanks again for your forbearance and patience about 'the book'. Thanks too to the fabulous author Nuala O'Connor who is so kind in steering me the right way in the world of publishing, to Katherine Lynch for her kind generosity and to my pal, therapist and confidante Fiona Hoban for her insight and sincere encouragement. Finally, infinite thanks and love to my Mam, my family and my friends.

'Don't shrink.
Don't puff up.
Just stand your sacred ground.'

Brené Brown

Contents

For my darling kiddos, Róisín & Muiris

Introduction

Every day children in schools all around the world eat their lunch in toilet cubicles; others spend entire mornings in class silently agonising about who might hang out with them at lunchtime; millions immediately panic when they hear the familiar ping from their mobile and they realise that yet another so-called friend has posted spiteful venom about them on social media.

As a psychotherapist, I felt compelled to write this book in response to the sheer number of people who come to me whose lives have been blighted by bullying. Parents come to me because they are devastated that their children are being bullied. Kids who are being bullied also come to me and the bewildered pain that often characterises the initial sessions is harrowing. Not only that, but I also often work with children who find the social aspect of their lives difficult – the kids who are hanging on the edges of the group. These kids feel they don't quite 'fit in' – and they aren't even sure they want to – but they live in a world obsessed with popularity, with sociability and with counting 'likes' on their social media.

It is estimated that approximately 10–15% of any given group of children repeatedly bully others while approximately 10–15% of children are repeatedly targeted by bullies. Although physical bullying decreases with age, on the other hand verbal, social and cyberbullying peaks between the ages of 10 and 15.[1] Thankfully, as teenagers grow older they bully less and usually by the time they leave school the prevalence of bullying is significantly reduced.

Although girls are more likely to use social bullying as a way to wield power over another while boys tend to use physical violence more often, it doesn't really matter whether the bullying is physical, social, emotional or cyber – bullying reaches deep into a person's psyche and shatters the sense of self. Girls might be subtler – using gossip and exclusion – while boys are more obvious and yet boys tend to bully more often and they keep at it longer.[2] The child who has been bullied often feels deep down that they have been viewed, judged and then stamped as not good enough and their trust in other people's goodness is destroyed. The thing about bullying is that the humiliation and shame is almost overwhelming. Each little kid who has been bullied thinks that this is their individual failure and they usually blame themselves. They may feel relieved and even vindicated 20 years later when they discover that it wasn't their fault, nor were they alone in their experience, but the anguish of being abandoned and humiliated by their peers at a crucial stage of development often leaves many long-term scars.

Within the counselling context, I often meet many children whose disdainful attitude towards the 'loners' and 'freaks' in their social domain is downright disturbing. When I challenge these otherwise considerate and kind kids, they tend to look bemused, shrug their shoulders and mindlessly dismiss the pain of their peers. Other bystanders wring their hands in concern but tend not to do anything that will actually help the target. Schools, usually more focused on children's education than their emotional well-being, tend to hope the exclusion or the bullying might be a molehill rather than a mountain and so they tend to underplay any bullying. The target is often so humiliated by the experience that they prefer to keep their head down and wish it all away. This is another reason why I wrote this book and the dismissive dehumanisation of other people's pain is one of the many issues involving bullying that I became determined to address.

The good news is that bullying can be combated. The bad news is that not enough people are educated about how to do this. This book intends to ensure that readers are fully equipped to handle any bullying that comes their way – no matter what their role is.

I work in a private practice in the midlands in Ireland and of the three second-level schools in the area, one of the schools appears to handle bullying very effectively, another does reasonably well, while the third school encounters bullying on an almost continuous basis. This is remarkable to me as the kids are all from mostly similar backgrounds. The difference is that this school minimises any bullying incidents or pretends that there is no bullying taking place, while the other two schools are, to a greater or lesser extent, willing to address the problem and take the necessary steps to deal with it.

This book explores the dark world of bullying and examines how and why some approaches are more successful than others. In this book, readers will learn about strategies that will combat bullying and exclusion. The reasons why people bully, why some personalities try to gain power over their peers, why some people are targeted more than others and why bystanders don't intervene are all examined. Different approaches are outlined so that targets can recover from their experiences and be able to move forward with confidence, self-awareness and self-acceptance.

Many parents and teachers deal with bullying by saying, 'Don't bully', or else 'Stand up to them' or 'Laugh it off'. Sadly, this advice seldom works and a much more comprehensive approach is needed to handle this complex issue. In addition, many parents tend to look the other way and pretend that bullying and social exclusion isn't happening the length and breadth of the country; then when it hits their own family they often feel isolated and disheartened by other people's lack of solidarity. After reading this book, readers will have a more complete understanding of these issues and an insight into how best to respond to bullying and complex social situations for preteens and teenagers.

There is no silver bullet. Insight, self-awareness and emotional intelligence aren't developed in a day, but kids who always feel on the edge of things, kids who kill time at their locker every day because they find the complex manoeuvrings of their peers difficult to deal with; these kids need to be helped to improve their social skills. It isn't appropriate to protect children from everything but, as a parent, it is our role to help our children when they need it. This book will help parents to support their kids in their quest to become bully-proof.

1

Defining bullying
What is and what isn't bullying?

*'First they ignore you, then they laugh at you,
then they fight you, then you win.'*

Mahatma Gandhi

'The first time things went wrong for me as a child was when I was bullied by my classmates'... 'I think everything began to fall apart when I got bullied as a kid'... 'I lost my self-confidence when I was a child and I fell out with my friends'... Variations of this sentence are being heard today and every day by counsellors and healers in therapy rooms all over the world. When I first worked as a psychotherapist, initially I was astonished by how many clients traced their first feelings of depression or anxiety or other mental health issues back to when they were bullied or excluded as a child, but as the years went by, I have now come to expect it.

According to Dr James O'Higgins Norman, director of the National Anti-Bullying Centre in Dublin City University, bullying can be described as 'repeated, aggressive behaviour by somebody with more power'.[3] Bullying, often deliberate and premeditated, tends to occur over a prolonged period of time. Bullying behaviour generally peaks at about age 12 while cyberbullying peaks at about age 15, but as anyone who has experienced a bullying boss will tell you, it certainly isn't confined to those years.[4] Bullies, of course, ultimately bear the responsibility for hurting others. However, if we wish to understand what is motivating bullies, then we must go beyond assigning blame and begin to properly analyse this area so that we can become much better at figuring out how to reduce the impact, intensity and frequency of bullying.

There are many different types of bullying, but the following analysis, taken from reachout.com, classifies the main types of bullying:

- Verbal – you're probably familiar with this one. It's name-calling, put-downs, mocking or threats. It can be face-to-face, written or, often, over the phone. It can also include sexual harassment.

- Physical – being punched, tripped, kicked or having your stuff stolen or damaged. It can also include sexual abuse.

- Social – being left out, ignored or having rumours spread about you. Often one of the hardest types of bullying to recognise and deal with.

- Psychological – this type of intimidation can also be hard to pin-point – dirty looks, stalking, manipulation, unpredictable reactions. It's often less direct than other types of bullying and you can feel like it's all in your head.

- Cyberbullying – being slagged off or harassed by email, text, on social networking sites or having your account hacked into. This is a new-ish and pretty tough type of bullying, because you can feel like there's no let-up from it.[5]

Why do some people bully?

Through examining nature, we can see that living things have the instinctual desire to gain some power and control over their environment so that they improve their chances of survival. When this need is met the body feels satisfied.

Many humans and animals also have, to a greater or lesser extent, an innate desire to herd together and create a pecking order. There is a valid reason why animals and humans tend to form groups. Weaker animals need the herd so that the stronger animals can protect them, and it is easier for animals to survive in a herd than all alone.

The term 'pecking order' (originally used to describe the hierarchical behaviour of chickens) describes the system of social organisation that many animal species, including humans, live by. Among animals, a chain of command can be very helpful as it clarifies the situation; everybody is assigned a role and so the group works together more effectively.

This instinctive need among animals and humans to create a pecking order is intensified during times of stress and conflict. And so, if our country is at war, we need our leaders to be very powerful if we are to win. Similarly, if a group is being attacked, the need for a pecking order becomes heightened. Sadly, many children often feel threatened because of the competitive elements in our society and so they tend to establish pecking orders everywhere they go – these kids feel the need for a leader or a couple of leaders because they feel insecure without one. Their insecurity compels them to create clearly defined roles for everyone in the group so that they can feel safer within the group.

It is the weaker animals that especially need the pack to be strong if they are to prosper and so they are often more defensive of the group than the stronger members. Weaker members are often hostile towards outsiders because they feel more threatened; they feel their position in the pack is at risk, they are concerned about the cohesiveness of the pack and they resist change for fear that they will be disadvantaged by it. If newcomers were allowed to easily come and go then the pack wouldn't be cohesive and strong. Consequently, sometimes it is the weaker sidekick who convinces the powerful bully to side-line and isolate the newbie in any group.

Of course, not many sidekicks are aware of their primal instinct to protect the purity of the pack. Instead, weaker members simply have an irresistible urge to see off the newcomers and to put them in their place – firmly outside the pack.

The reality of a pecking order among little boys became very clear to me recently when my six-year-old boy started soccer training. I was simply amazed how often my gentle little boy was suddenly embroiled in fistfights with other kids on the pitch. During training sessions a minor disagreement would have boys knocking the heads off one another quicker than you could say 'pecking order'. My boy, who was the newest kid on the block, seemed to be in a handful of fights during *every* training session for the first few weeks. A few months in and the boys seemed to have established who's who and there are very few outbreaks of violence nowadays. Meanwhile, my eight-year-old daughter – a significantly more assertive person than my son – has never, to my knowledge, been involved in a fistfight.

Although the gender gap is shrinking every day, it still remains the case that girls tend to establish a pecking order in a more subtle and guarded manner. When my daughter, Róisín, first went to dance class there was an intensely silent examination of each girl's clothes, demeanour, attractiveness and general popularity so that the pecking order could be established. Now that everyone knows who they are and their relative position on the social totem pole, the girls can get on with enjoying each other's company and learning how to dance. However, if anyone decides to act out of character in this dance class, then I have no doubt that intense stares and comments will put the imprudent girl back in her box very quickly.

Human nature and our competitive culture

Psychologists agree that all humans – every one of us – have an inborn emotional need for power or status of some kind. This need can vary across a spectrum from a very high to a very low need depending on the person. For some people their need for power is relatively low and can be easily met – for example, the child who feels satisfyingly powerful when they ride a bike or learn to play a game with their friends. However, other children have a more developed need for power and they tend to try to dominate any given situation. Children like this often have ambitious and powerful personalities and they can be very competitive. These kids with a high need for power often like to win because they have a stronger need to appear in control and they like to be the top dog.

The problem with the varying human need for power is that because of the limited natural resources on the planet, people with a strong need for power can tend to consume those who are less inclined to seek domination. Not only that, but our limited resources mean that there is always a certain level of competition going on in the world – not everyone can be rich – and so it is often those with the highest need for power, those who are most willing to fight for ascendancy and 'beat' everyone else, who are most likely to end up rich.

Our tendency to herd together is often finely balanced with our propensity to compete with members of our group for limited resources. The inhabitants of some communities won't survive unless they depend on their neighbours, and so, in these communities, towns and villages, a supportive and co-operative culture is nurtured. However, people who live in wealthier countries usually don't need to rely upon others to survive – they can get by just fine without depending on the village – and these people usually have a strong need to protect what they have already gathered.

This is arguably why people who are wealthier have a more individualistic outlook and tend to satisfy their need for power by protecting what they have, by ensuring others don't rise as high as they do and by competing with everyone else in their circle. Oliver James' polemical book *Status Anxiety* further details how and why the more materialistic and commercially driven societies tend to be more competitive, aggressive, individualistic, selfish and bullying.

To thrive in life, according to Western ideology, we must 'beat' everyone else. But we can't all beat everyone else and so there are many who fall victim to the 'winner-takes-all' belief. Many adults today teach children the misguided message that beating everyone else is the most impressive thing they can do. The problem with this is that in a world obsessed with success, with beating your opponents, with becoming 'the best', we are inadvertently creating a culture of bullying. Popular shows like *Britain's Got Talent* or *The Apprentice* tend to glorify bullies and a whole slew of video games from *Call of Duty* to *Clash of Clans* glorify violence in the name of entertainment. The rise of charismatic leaders who are also perceived as bullies, such as Vladimir Putin or Donald Trump, is another indication that these days we tend to give more respect to powerful bullies than we do to gentler, more reflective people. If influential adults encourage this 'winner-takes-all' attitude then it is unrealistic to expect children not to attempt to gain ascendancy over whoever they can – and, sadly, the easiest person to target is often the one kid in the room who especially needs compassion and gentleness.

Social media, although designed to bring us together, also drives us apart as we continuously count our 'likes' and our 'friends' and quantify our social standing by comparing ourselves to others every time we go on social media. Even the education system whereby children enter college promotes the 'winner-takes-all' ideology. The system of entry into third-level education is structured so that every candidate is competing against their peers, so if you just happen to be in a year where there are an unusual number of clever swots then you will undoubtedly find it a good deal harder to get into your preferred university course.

Compared to even fifty years ago, most of us in the Western world are relatively wealthy; it is unlikely that we will starve to death, contract a disease from malnutrition or find ourselves homeless with no shelter. But, rather than rejoicing in our good fortune, the human instinct for power motivates us to further control our environment, to protect our wealth and to seek further riches, better holidays and more 'stuff'.

The problem with our focus on 'stuff' and success is that it creates a harder society; a society that accepts power as a 'better' quality.

Children who are bullied are more likely to 'pass it on' and families that accept bullying as an effective form of getting what you want are naturally more likely to produce children who bully. These families are also, unfortunately, more likely to produce more people who are targeted by bullies as the gentler personalities within the family have become accustomed to being targeted.

'My father was a bully. He punched, kicked, roared and screamed until he got his way. My mother was a doormat and I made the conscious decision never to allow anyone treat me the way my father treated my mother. In many ways it was inevitable that I would become a bully. I had dyslexia and I was useless in school but I was determined not to be treated badly by anyone. So it was a case of shoot first before they shot me. I bullied the "swots" mercilessly. I slagged them, imitated their voices and physically hurt them at every opportunity.

I remember in primary school one unfortunate boy shat his pants in school and I kicked his arse all the way home. The excrement all went up his back and down his trousers until it spilled out. Poor kid, he was a couple of years younger than me. I knew everyone was wary of me and it felt good — I felt powerful.

It wasn't until I was all grown up and my own little girl was in school and she was bullied that I realised the harm I had caused. I've undergone a transformation since then but you could say that karma has caught up with me as my little girl seems to be filled with self-loathing as a result of all the bullying that she has experienced.'

Shay, 41

The neuroscience of bullying

The ground-breaking work that has been done on the brain in recent years has inspired many new theories on bullying. It is now known that the amygdala in our brain serves to trigger our 'fight or flight' response. Some psychologists argue that a third and fourth response can also be triggered – 'fight or flight, freeze or appease'. When we believe we are being attacked – whether by a mugger in a dark alley, by a lion in the jungle or by an aggressive, power-seeking kid on the first day of soccer training – we tend to act first and think later. Some of us stand and fight, some of us run for the hills, some of us freeze completely and some of us try to appease the aggressor. It is only later on that we tend to analyse and try to figure out whether we behaved correctly or not.

If we take into account the animal instinct to establish a herd or a community that makes each member feel stronger, and combine it with our knowledge about the amygdala, it soon becomes even more understandable why the weaker, more insecure individuals – the sidekicks – often encourage their stronger and more confident peers – the potential bullies – to bring down and destroy the 'outsider'. Weaker individuals are more easily threatened and they feel a greater need than stronger individuals to strengthen the group. When the weaker individual in a group feels threatened, their amygdala is triggered and they immediately go into 'fight' mode because they wish to reassure themselves that they have the powerful personality of the bully to back up their position. Sadly, the target often goes into 'flight' mode and the sidekicks and the bullies thereby enjoy a quick shot of power and so they often return to the target in a bid to repeat the experience.

There is some good news, though, because further research on the brain shows us that humans have further developed their response to the amygdala with the prefrontal lobes behind the forehead. This gives humans the opportunity to attempt to persuade, placate or outwit their adversary and so emotionally intelligent people can often talk their way out of a bullying situation as they can more easily understand what is driving the situation and can figure out what they need to say to placate them. It is this ability to box clever that can help the target of bullies to move beyond bullying to a more secure position in the social group.

The difference between bullying and conflict

There is a growing tendency for people to cry 'bully' when in reality no bullying is taking place. Many people feel that the word 'bullying' has been hijacked and its meaning has been abused and diluted through flippant overuse. This linguistic creep means that it is not always clear just who the bully is and who the victim is; and so everyone loses when the word 'bully' is misused and overused. It skews the general public's view of bullies and creates feelings of outrage and sympathy on behalf of wrongly accused so-called bullies.

Lack of knowledge about what bullying actually is further conflates the issue of bullying. Both my children are prone to shout 'bully' whenever they get into conflict. They are children of their generation and so it has been drilled into them at school, at their activities and from everyone else that bullying is bad and it is a quick method to get the full attention of the supervising adult. And so randomly, from the back of the car, these squabbling siblings suddenly shout 'You're a bully!' in a bid for Mammy's attention.

Bullying is meanness from someone with more power than you that is repeated over a period of time. Teasing isn't bullying;

taunting isn't even bullying – although it's unkind and it can be traumatising, the taunting would have to be repeated over a period of time by someone with more power to be described as bullying. Having a sustained conflict or disagreement with someone also isn't bullying. Neither can being mean or unkind be classed as bullying, unless it happens repeatedly and the perpetrator has more power than the target.

Gina came to me for counselling as she had been very distressed about accusations of bullying from another student in her class. Gina came from a politically involved family and she loved debating thorny issues with anyone who would engage. An atheist and a scientist, Gina had become inflamed by the fact that one of her schoolmates, Pauline, was a committed Catholic who also held Creationist views. The situation was further complicated because Gina and Pauline were also rivals for the pole position in the class. Gina became like a rabid bloodhound baiting Pauline into a discussion about evolution and then blinding her with scientific theory. Gina enjoyed every moment of it. Pauline dreaded it and began to pretend to be sick so she could stay off school.

Pauline's mother called the principal and demanded that something be done about Gina's bullying. Gina was hauled into the principal's office and was horrified to learn that she was being accused of being a bully – Gina thought she was engaging in intellectual discourse! Although willing to attend counselling, Gina felt bewildered by this turn of events and was relieved when I explained to her that if a person is willing to engage in reasoned debate without tipping over the line into name-calling or silencing the other person then they are generally not bullying – they may merely be impassioned. Some people are very opinionated and they enjoy challenging and debating issues with others. Some people don't like this type of person; they find them confrontational and tiresome and so they should probably keep their distance from them. Then again, other people don't like the type of person who keeps their opinions to themselves and refuses to engage in debate.

Tackling gossip and teasing

If your child comes to you worried about gossip or teasing that is going on in their lives, first of all you need to take the child seriously. Don't dismiss, downplay or use humour in this deeply vulnerable moment.

Listen carefully to your child. Ask open-ended questions so that you can ascertain exactly how your child is feeling, e.g. 'Am I right in thinking that you are particularly annoyed because they are doing all this behind your back?' Be prepared for your child to become irritated when you don't get it quickly enough; apologise and plod on haplessly anyway until you completely understand the situation.

Empathise with your child. Put yourself in their shoes for a moment. This might be very painful for you and so many parents tend to brush over this bit but it will give you a deeper understanding of their pain and you won't be so inclined to minimise the situation in the future. You can empathise with your child by using the exact words that they use; if the teenager says it is 'horrendous' then make sure when you are clarifying that you use the word 'horrendous' instead of similar words such as 'horrible' or 'disastrous'. By using the words that they use to describe their emotions you are learning to see it from their perspective.

Be prepared to spend a lot of time discussing the pros and cons of the next step. This can be discussed with the child, but perhaps not only with the child and not always in front of the child. Forums such as mumsnet.com can give perspective, as closer friends on your local social media groups can tend towards hysteria, righteousness and an unhealthy desire to be involved in a bit of drama.

Over-protected 'cotton wool kids'

In this era of over-protected 'cotton wool kids', many children are so accustomed to looking to the nearest adult to rescue them that when they reach their teen years they haven't yet developed any ability to look after themselves. In my work as a psychotherapist I often meet these innocent and much-loved kids who haven't yet had the opportunity to learn resilience, self-protection or well-developed social skills.

My previous book *Cotton Wool Kids* explores how many kids today haven't had the opportunity to learn how to handle problems, big or small, on their own and so they often ask their parents or their teacher to help when they are being bullied – with the full expectation that the adults will save the day as they have always done before. It can be very disconcerting for these children when they enter secondary school and they realise that it is suddenly no longer appropriate or possible for the grown-ups to step in and fight their battles – indeed, many of them feel like they have fallen from a cliff without a safety net when parents and teachers offer strategies that will help them but ultimately expect the child to sort it out themselves.

But these kids can't sort it out themselves – they haven't had any practice at it yet.

These tweens and teens have no experience or know-how when it comes to conflict and so, sometimes, conflict that can and should be managed easily can tip into bullying as the offender realises that the target runs to Mammy every time they are upset. The gaucheness of the cotton wool kid then becomes another reason to tease the child. The target might wrongly believe that their parents or teachers will stop the bullying and they often don't understand that their power really lies within. If parents don't teach their children how to handle conflict or difficult people then the child won't be fully equipped to become a healthy, functioning adult when they leave their teen years.

> *When Rónán, 13, was in primary school, he could easily cope with any negativity he received from his schoolmates; he simply went up and told the teacher and the teacher generally ensured that everyone would play nicely. However, this system didn't work so well when Rónán moved from primary to secondary school.*
>
> *At the start of first year, a boy called Josh kept teasing Rónán about his hairstyle and so Rónán (instead of dealing directly with Josh and telling him to lay off) did what he had been taught to do — he requested help from the supervising adults. But the teasing was mild and the teacher advised Rónán to handle it himself.*
>
> *Josh and his friends soon realised that Rónán had 'snitched' on him and it hadn't worked. As a direct result of this, they upped the ante. They began calling him 'rat' whenever he walked by. Rónán refused to look at them and stared down at the ground whenever they taunted him. Josh and his friends thought that this was hilarious and began doing all sorts of things in a bid to make Rónán react. Rónán, not knowing what else to do, still didn't react*

— never realising that this had become part of the game for Josh and his group.

At a loss, Rónán asked his mother to help. His mother duly contacted the school and was told that Rónán needed to learn to fight his own battles. Eventually, Rónán ended up in my office for counselling and he told me the whole story. What had started as a very small event had continued unchecked until Rónán's life in his new school was being ruined by mindless bullying. Rónán and I worked together and, over time, Rónán learned to handle the bullies with forethought and emotional intelligence (see Chapters 8 & 9). Josh and his pals became less entertained by Rónán as he was no longer responding in a way that made them laugh and so they moved on to other means of entertainment.

One day, as Rónán and I were reflecting on the damage caused to his psyche by the months of bullying in his first year of secondary school, Rónán suddenly exploded, 'God, I wish I had just handled it right the first couple of times Josh slagged me! I needlessly endured months of misery because I just didn't know how to respond!'

Why we have become so sensitive to imagined hurts? Why do we choose to dwell on one negative remark and tend to cast aside the positive remarks? This book aims to give a comprehensive view on bullying and so the increase of inappropriate accusations of bullying and the culture of offence needs to be thoroughly explored.

Many of us, in certain circumstances, can end up playing the victim. Generally, we do this in a bid to have more control of a situation or to try to cope with a situation. If this doesn't work out successfully for us then we may learn more helpful coping strategies. However, if playing the victim does bring about the desired outcome, many people can fall into this way of behaving without knowing any better. We will look at this in more detail in Chapter 4.

A 'cry-bully' is the oxymoronic name for people who play the victim in a bid to dominate any given situation. The controversial journalist Julie Burchill succinctly describes the cry-bully as 'a hideous hybrid of victim and victor, weeper and walloper'.[6] In the old days the bully kicked sand in the face of the victim and we all rooted for the victim to triumph. But it's all much more complicated than that now, and nowadays when bullying is mentioned, wary caution is the most common reaction as people try to figure out the full story. This became very evident to me when I told colleagues that I was writing a book about bullying and many people contacted me with the express request that I include the rising issue of inappropriate accusations of bullying.

I often give talks in schools and organisations around the country and just recently I was asked to give a talk in a certain school where there was a serious problem with bullying. I was advised beforehand that a child – let's call her 'Niamh' – was bullying many of her peers and it was for this reason that I was drafted in. I had barely put up my first slide when the first sob came from Niamh. To my utter amazement, Niamh's sobs continued unabated throughout the talk as she explained loudly at every opportunity how she was a victim of bullying. The nonplussed hostility from everyone else in the room demonstrated clearly what Niamh's peers thought of her crocodile tears, and yet Niamh was obviously in great anguish and evidently thought of herself as a victim of bullying.

Sadly, because bullying gets so much instant attention, some bullies pose as victims of bullying in a bid to gain power and control over a situation. In the film *Mean Girls*, the character of Regina George goes a bit mad when she loses her power over everyone and poses as a victim of bullying to her school principal. Regina shows the principal a book that she herself had made, filled with pages of all sorts of terrible things about everyone in the school – including herself. Regina does this to gain control over the situation by posing as a victim of bullying. Mad perhaps, but strangely common.

2

Complicated relationships
Frenemies and power plays

*'Wishing to be friends is quick work, but
friendship is a slow-ripening fruit.'*

Aristotle

C hildren are, of course, new to the game of life, and they tend
to make friends quickly, easily and naively. This is all well
and good when they are very young; however, as children
grow older (usually from about nine years onwards), they begin to
discriminate between their friends.

This can become a very troublesome aspect of childhood for the
type of child who finds it difficult to understand the complexities
and subtleties of the social world. And so, some kids – kids who
tend to fall in and out of friendships, kids who have difficulties
making or keeping friends and kids who frequently find themselves
enmeshed in complicated power plays – often need extra help and
support with maintaining positive relationships. Although parents
can't make their children suddenly become popular, they can build
and develop their child's emotional intelligence so that the child
becomes more aware and better able to anticipate the impact of

certain behaviour. Simply by learning better social skills, these k̲
will find their social life easier and more manageable.

Psychosocial stages and personality types

It is when tweens and teenagers begin to form their identities and
become more socially sensitive that they often tend to become
incredibly conscious of the social standing of their friends. They
become afraid to be friends with someone who isn't pre-approved
by the pack because in doing so they might inadvertently lower
their own stock. It is during the socially volatile early teen years
that kids most desperately want to be part of a tribe and many of
them will do almost anything to fit into whatever random group
they find themselves in.

Erik Erikson's world-renowned psychosocial stages of human
development show us why it is that teenagers become inordinately
involved with their peers in secondary school. From the age of 12
to 18 normally developing humans psychologically begin to move
away from their families and begin to figure out who they really
are. As teenagers are finding their identity, their peers begin to
replace their family as their chief influence. This is why the intense
focus on social standing is a natural part of the teenage years, but
it is important to help the child keep perspective as it can be a
very cruel time for everyone involved. Many teachers report that
2nd year in secondary school is emotional carnage as the students
become almost obsessed with their social status. Fortunately, this
all calms down by the time they have grown up enough to go on to
third level (the bad news is that by then they will become obsessed
with finding 'the one'). See the table on Erikson's psychosocial
stages for more details.[7]

Stage	Psychosocial Crisis	Basic Virtue	Age
1	Trust vs. mistrust	Hope	Infancy (0 to 1½)
2	Autonomy vs. shame	Will	Early childhood (1½ to 3)
3	Initiative vs. guilt	Purpose	Play age (3 to 5)
4	Industry vs. inferiority	Competency	School age (5 to 12)
5	Ego identity vs. role confusion	Fidelity	Adolescence (12 to 18)
6	Intimacy vs. isolation	Love	Young adulthood (18 to 40)
7	Generativity vs. stagnation	Care	Adulthood (40 to 65)
8	Ego integrity vs. despair	Wisdom	Maturity (65+)

Some children, especially those who haven't formed a strong identity, can yield to whatever way the wind blows and might more easily get along with everyone. Other children form a strong identity at a young age and so they can find it harder to mix socially with different personality types. It is often the children with stronger personalities who find their schooldays that bit harder as they find it more difficult to roll with the punches – they can't just put aside their likes and dislikes without rebelling on some level.

Some children are naturally easy-going and so will always get along with the crowd. Many parents dearly wish that their children were more easy-going – not selfishly, but because many parents remember with horror those who struggled socially during their own teenage years, and so they naturally hope that their children are well-liked, find friends easily and don't have to face any of that cruelty. This is why being easy-going is often considered a very desirable trait to have; it is also much easier on a day-to-day basis to live with someone who is easy-going.

Well, if all your children are easy-going and find it easy to make friends, you are unlikely to be reading this book and so we can safely assume that your life is a bit more complicated than that. However, it is important to point out (albeit this is coming from a person who isn't particularly easy-going herself) that although being easy-going is handy when you're a teenager and going through the psychosocial stage where popularity is everything, as we grow up being easy-going is not necessarily the very best thing to be.

I know two children very well. One is intense, loyal, passionate and volatile; the other is easy-going, flexible, likeable and calm. All of these traits have worth and value; however, most adults prefer the easy-going child. (Well, they would, wouldn't they?) I am an intense person and I would just like to take this opportunity to give a shout out for the more 'challenging' (or 'difficult') among us.

Easy-going people tend not to challenge people or the status quo and they prefer to conform and comply; this is why it is so much easier for an adult to be in the company of an easy-going child. However, on the other hand, an easy-going person is less likely to do anything significantly useful or worthwhile – they often don't have the commitment, passion or the dogged determination that is generally required for a person to achieve the extraordinary. Instead, easy-going people tend to be a force for good in another way because their presence often impacts the world in a positive manner, and yet the passionate people can also be a force for good – for it is the intense and passionate people who are motivated to commit to changing the world. If we look to history (or even look among our own family) we soon see that we need intense, loyal, passionate and volatile people just as much as we need calm, funny and easy-going people and so, thankfully, all God's creatures have a place in the choir!

Popularity and the social hierarchy

Most children, by the time they are 11 years old, say they are part of a friendship group or clique and an interesting hierarchy among children in a classroom setting has been identified.[8]

Approximately one-third of students are in the dominant popular group. This group or clique may (depending on the environment) engage in a lot of nasty political behaviour so as to maintain or enhance their social status.

About one-tenth of children are in the 'wannabe' group. These kids hang around the edges of the popular group hoping desperately to get the nod so they can join the cool clique. They usually get enough crumbs of approval from the head table to keep them hooked, but they rarely gain full acceptance.

About one-half of students occupy the middle ground. This involves smaller, independent friendship groups, where the emphasis is on being loyal, kind and supportive of each other. These kids often dislike the popular kids, because they see them as unfriendly and standoffish, but they also look down on less popular kids. It is these kids that the involved parent of an unhappily socialised child needs to try to identify and work towards – but remember, your child might be so dazzled by the 'cool kids' that they can be dismissive of this crowd.

About one-tenth of the students are socially isolated from every group. These children are most at risk for being targets of bullying.

> *'When I think about my schooldays I want to recoil in horror. I was such a quiet little wimp that slavishly followed whatever I thought the popular girls followed. We all wore the same clothes, the same hair and the same make-up with tiny little differences between us. We went shopping together and the girls effectively approved everything I bought. I liked the music that the girls liked, I liked the films that the girls liked — I literally had no mind of my own. Eventually, thank God, I moved away from the girls when I went to college and I gained a mind of my own.'*
>
> *Cathy, 37*

Is it risky for kids to try to become more popular? Yes it is; research shows that while already-popular kids will get away with aggressive tactics in a bid to win more popularity, unpopular kids won't.[9] On the other hand, there is no serious harm in less popular kids learning to conform, on some level, to peer culture such as clothing, slang or musical tastes. Although it might be tempting for parents to dismiss their children's concerns about popularity, it's really not very fair to do this, as for tweens and teens, it is only natural to be focused upon your social standing. This is exactly where teenagers should be in terms of brain development – moving away from the hold their parents have over them and becoming more interested in their status among their peers. So maybe, in certain volatile circumstances, you should allow them – even, God save us, encourage them – to get the new Hollister hoodie for their birthday.

Few of us arrive on earth with our social status fixed, and so, as we grow up, we become conscious of the world beyond our family and we then begin to ascertain our place in the world. By the time we get to adulthood most of us have learned to accept our positions and live happily among others, or else we move our social position to somewhere that makes a better fit (although it must be said that some people choose to become consumed by bitter regret over their childhood status and never manage to move beyond the start they had in life). It is appropriate for teens and tweens to explore where they fit best on the social totem pole so that they can then decide whether it is a good fit or whether they need to change their world.

Some parents are delighted when they realise that their child is popular, but once popularity has been established, the child isn't home and dry as this situation is constantly being re-configured as different kids vie for top dog placement. Besides (as many parents have seen to their shock and horror when they throw a birthday party and their little darling turns into some sort of crazed despot), some children aren't mature enough to handle the power that popularity brings. Indeed, many kids get a rush of blood to the head when they realise that they have power and they lose the plot entirely.

Relational aggression

Relational aggression is when friendship is used as a weapon in a bid to control peers and can be seen in social interactions between children as young as three years old.[10] Until relatively recently, this term was largely unknown but now schools, parents and media are taking notice of this destructive way of behaving. When physical aggression isn't tolerated, controlling children often turn to relational aggression to get their way and so they demand of their friends, 'Do this or I won't be your friend any more'. This can be subtle and effectively communicated through dark looks, silent treatment and body language.

It's very difficult for a child to try to explain relational aggression to their parents or the teachers. Lara was ten years old when she tried to explain to me how she was being cold-shouldered by the girls in her group. She couldn't articulate the words properly although she was desperately trying to: 'They keep looking at me meanly and whispering ... They turn their backs to me when I try and join the circle so I'm left outside it while they're whispering ... They write notes to each other about me.' Lara had already tried to tell her mother about the situation but it hadn't gone well: 'I talk to my Mom about everything but when I tell her about the mean girls she gets really annoyed and tells me to ignore them. *But I can't.* It's too hard. And I don't like making my Mom mad so I don't really tell her any more.'

The problem with all this is that a ten-year-old girl just hasn't the language, social context, subtlety, perspective or public consciousness to fully understand what's going on. And this is exactly why and how many young girls (and it is mostly girls) move from feeling helpless and powerless to engaging in bitter self-recrimination, self-blame and self-loathing.

However, as children grow older and more socially insightful, they begin to see relational aggression for the manipulation it really is. Thankfully, by the time the teenagers move into their late teens the social power of these so-called cool kids is diluted as teenagers begin to form real and lasting friendships.

How to handle difficult friendships

Don't alienate yourself by mindlessly criticising your child's friends! Because we've been in the world longer, many parents can identify troublesome aspects of certain friendships before their kids can. It is essential that parents use whatever emotional intelligence they have to ensure they don't paint their child into a corner. If the child feels they have to defend their friend from the parents' attacks this can prolong the friendship for many months and even years. Parents need to understand both the positive and the negative aspects of each friendship before they are fit to comment on the relationship. If you can't wrap your head around a particular friendship then you might need, for the sake of your child, to explore the positive aspect of the friendship a good deal more before you say or do anything at all. Timing is everything and it is important that you don't mindlessly criticise your child's friends at the wrong time. It is much more helpful to bite your lip and wait until the time is right to point out certain aspects of the friendship that are troublesome while at the same time agreeing that none of us is perfect. Depending on how destructive the relationship is, some parents need to show faith that their child, with some helpful added insight from their parents, will eventually make their own mind up about difficult friendships.

I have personal experience of this as I remember well my parents taking 'agin' one of my friends. But what my parents didn't know, and what I wasn't able to articulate at the time, was that I needed this 'friend' for a whole raft of reasons. I was actually very aware that she wasn't very nice but I was also aware enough to know that I needed her for complicated social reasons — her approval meant that I wasn't ostracised by the 'cool group'. My life was hard enough at the time and my parents making it difficult for me to see this 'friend' made things even harder.

The controlling friend

The controlling friend often has the typical traits of the 'pure bully' (see Chapter 3). This person is often powerful and popular. They try to control the group and they try to control their friends. Many people who are being controlled by a friend have a very ambivalent attitude to the situation; they dislike being controlled but they believe that, deep down, the controlling friend knows better than they do and so they have every right to control them. Sadly, many children are drawn to these controlling friends. They can be fun, socially savvy, exciting and popular and they often have many others in their thrall.

Parents, as with all friendships, but particularly with this type of friendship, need to be ultra-sensitive to the situation. They will probably need to help their children to develop their emotional intelligence (see Chapters 8 & 9) if they are to emerge unscathed from the friendship.

This type of friendship is fraught with problems and, in many ways, should be handled as if it's bullying (see Chapter 8) – although there may not be any need to contact the school or the parents in question.

Humour and teasing

Unfortunately, many power-based friendships are offset with humour. The powerful people and the sidekicks in the group often develop a quick wit so that they can use this shamelessly to garner more power and popularity. We all enjoy the feeling of power and satisfaction when people laugh at our jokes, and for bullies or ringleaders who are particularly driven to seek power, this gives them a heady feeling that can be very addictive. If the environment is boring and unchallenging or, equally, if the environment is over-competitive and threatening and kids need light relief, many can 'fall into' bullying simply looking for distraction. When this is the case, not only do the authorities need to empower the targets with more insight, control the rampant viciousness in the bullies and teach awareness and moral engagement to everybody concerned, they also need to curb the prevalent boredom and tension in a more positive manner (see Chapter 6).

Humour is often used to prevent boredom but casual arguments are another, more destructive way to alleviate boredom. Minor tiffs are common in friendships and they can be an opportunity for learning to compromise and how to agree to disagree. Yet some children are more prone to squabbling than others and they might need to learn some more about problem-solving and managing conflict.

Most of us can easily recognise good teasing; it's affectionate, everyone is in on the joke and nobody feels bad about themselves. Bad teasing can come from the same spirit as good teasing but the teaser often goes too far, pushes the wrong button or highlights something that the target didn't especially want to get highlighted. In this case, the target needs to honour their own feelings and nicely ask them to stop teasing as it is embarrassing.

It is the downright evil teasing that causes the most upset. This is when the villains who live higher up in the pecking order focus their attention on an embarrassing aspect of the target's life and they go for the jugular. The real word for this is 'taunting'; however, bullies trivialise it by calling it 'teasing' or 'slagging'. Tragically, this taunting can be very witty and very funny (in a cruel kind of way). So the bystanders – and even the target – can find themselves laughing at the pure comedy of the taunting, even when they really don't want to be part of the nasty behaviour. The difference between teasing and taunting is demonstrated on the next page.

Teasing vs. Taunting

Teasing

- ✓ Tries to make everyone laugh
- ✓ Doesn't intend to cause offence
- ✓ Fundamentally light-hearted
- ✓ The teaser can swap roles with ease and be teased themselves
- ✓ Stops immediately if offence is caused

Taunting

- ✓ Laughs at, not with, the target
- ✓ Intends to upset
- ✓ Often involves humiliating or demeaning comments thinly disguised as jokes
- ✓ Based upon an imbalance of power
- ✓ Continues despite evident distress

'I'm embarrassed to admit it but I was a bully at school. I didn't enjoy school because it was very intense yet very boring and we were always looking for a bit of craic to relieve the relentless stress. Looking back, all I can say is that I kind of fell into the bullying, and, once I started bullying, I pretended to myself that the target deserved it. It was also very funny to our puerile minds.

There was one girl in the school who wasn't liked. She was a know-it-all and a tell-tale. She had absolutely no sense of humour and it was for that reason we fell into bullying her. At first we would mock her and pretend to be really impressed by her vast knowledge and her perfect grades. She would swell up like a balloon and deliver long lectures to us about the life cycle of a frog while we would pretend to be rapt. It was all harmless enough at that stage but as time went on it became nastier.

We used to call her Nora Batty because she looked so old-fashioned. And we would play cruel games on her by pretending to arrange to meet her and then not turn up but instead hide and watch her waiting for us anxiously, all dressed up and nowhere to go. The thing about 'Nora' was that she couldn't hide her feelings and so, in our world of cool, it seemed so funny to see the hot indignation on her guileless face.

Then we started picking on her family and sending pizzas and stuff to be delivered to their family home. It all sounds so stupid now, but honestly the look of moral outrage on their faces was really funny. The family had no social savvy at all. For all their knowledge, they could never seem to figure out pretty obvious traps. They used to ring the police over the pizza deliveries and they were probably just laughed at by the Gardaí. We just did it out of boredom, and the more they rose to the occasion, the funnier it all got to our teenage sensibility.

I remember one girl putting used sanitary towels in her schoolbag while Nora Batty was bent over furiously writing in some exam. They had been taken from the waste disposal in the toilets. I remember watching this unfold and thinking "it's all gone a bit sick now" but it's hard to explain how the whole thing just took a life of its own. The only way to relieve the boredom and have some laughs in that horrible school was to make Nora Batty lose the head.'

Paul, 35

Frenemies and toxicity

Some friendships are toxic. Parents tend to be horrified by the arrival of the 'frenemy' into their child's life and yet as the saying goes, 'To be old and wise you must first be young and stupid'. If parents try to get in the way of their child learning how to handle the toxic friend they may merely be postponing and prolonging this painful lesson.

Frenemies are enemies disguised as friends. These are often relationships characterised by rivalry and resentment, and frenemies can be masters at backhanded compliments. They rarely rejoice in each other's good fortune and instead spend their time undermining each other.

Susie was a lovely ten-year-old girl whose mother, Emma, came to me in distress as her daughter was choosing to play with a girl who treated her badly. No matter how badly her powerful friend treated her, Susie would delightedly trot back into place once the friend was nice to her again. Eventually Emma agreed with Susie that they would silently bestow 'black marks' to the frenemy every time she treated Susie badly. After 20 black marks were counted, Susie had built up a better awareness of the pattern and became less impressed with her frenemy's behaviour. Susie eventually befriended another girl, Heather, who was also being mistreated and they began to stick together in the schoolyard — much to Emma's delight. As Euripides said, 'Friends show their love in times of trouble, not in happiness,' and, over time, Heather and Susie became great friends.

How your child feels after spending time with their friend is a good indication of the health of the relationship. If your child appears downcast, it can be effective to ask probing questions that highlight exactly what it is that has distressed them – it may take clever questioning to encourage your child to open up, but if you are skilful and subtle, this can be a great opportunity for parents to guide their child towards a greater emotional insight.

While the classic 'frenemy' relationship is bad enough, if your child is hopelessly devoted to another who is more an enemy than a friend, it can be difficult for the parent to stand idly by as their child is spitefully used and abused by another.

The 'frenemy' can be both very kind and very aggressive. They are skilled at understanding other people but they use this to manipulate any given situation. This type of person tends to dole out enough kindness to the right people at the right time to keep them hooked, and then, on the other hand, they dole out enough meanness to maintain their social power and keep others off balance. Nice.

When the frenemy has captivated your child

Calmly point out the pattern. Kids tend to live in the moment so it is the parent's role to point out the pattern that exists in this friendship. It will be easier to do this if, at first, you point it out concerning another friend and not your own child. The parent needs to be calm and gentle — impassioned sermons will turn your child against you and not their powerful friend!

Ask thought-provoking questions and try to keep your tone curious and open-minded — you will defeat the point of the exercise if you are accusatory.

'What have you noticed about the way Sarah treats Heather?'

'How do you think Heather feels around Sarah?'

'Why do you think Heather keeps trying to be friends with Sarah?'

'Do you know the way Sarah speaks meanly about Heather now that they're fighting — do you think she might speak about you like that when you have fought with her?'

'Now that Sarah and Heather are friends again, do you think it will last this time?'

Prepare your child for the next blow-up. Telling your child not to be friends with the all-powerful frenemy is unlikely to work; however, you can prepare them for the next row by being the mature adult who keeps an eye on the ebbs and flows of the relationship. There are often signs that the blow-up is coming and you can point these out to your child as a pattern of behaviour that often involves 'Sarah'. When your child has learned to read the signs leading up to a blow-up then they have learned a certain level of emotional intelligence that will help them in future relationships.

Ask your child how many times they are prepared to accept being treated badly until they walk away. Get your child to give a number; it might be twenty or it might be five — the point is that the power is in your child's hands. Your child can silently give the frenemy a 'ticket' every time they are cruel — the parent can help by ensuring each incident is noted and then when the frenemy reaches the allotted number of tickets your child is free to behave as they wish. The parent can, in the meantime, be reassured that the friendship will have changed as their child gains awareness. Your child may choose to walk away but if they don't, they will at least have acquired greater emotional insight about the pattern of behaviour.

Teen drama, gossip and hormones

Today, in teen world, where 'likes' on social media are counted, contrasted and compared, popularity is the royal road to success. Teen drama erupts because different kids are vying to be top dog and in their bid for presidency, they often create fights and tension on the way. The problem with this drama is that often the potential top dogs are so busy fighting for prestige that they cruelly hurt weaker chains in the social group in their bid for a quick display of superiority. If a child is caught up in a situation where 'teen drama' is rampant, the best thing a parent can do is remember that parenting is a long-term game and begin the process of helping to develop their child's emotional intelligence so they can understand better both their own motivations and their friends'.

Gossip can be so interesting that, just like comedic teasing, decent people can be lured into gossiping from the pure drama of the story. I understand the attraction that gossip can hold; I, too, have read the celeb magazines and I, too, have binged on rubbish from the *Daily Mail*. But when we allow other people's disasters to be our entertainment, are we making a deal with the devil as one day our own disaster might be lunchtime fodder for other people?

Sometimes gossip is harmless enough; people are simply discussing any given situation and giving their own personal take on it – indeed, it can even lead to interesting conversations. However, if a person is feeling insecure then gossip can destroy lives.

If a child tells a parent that there is gossip going around the school about them, it is very important that the parent doesn't dismiss it with some sort of trite 'sticks and stones' or other dross. The intense maelstrom of emotion that characterises any school filled with children, tweens and/or emotional teens means that perspective is scarce and melodrama is plentiful. For a child, today is everything and what is happening today has an extraordinary level of importance in their world: even tomorrow can feel like the distant future.

It is much more helpful for the parent to be gentle with the humiliated child who feels forced to go to their parent because of the gossiping. If your child, however offhandedly, mentions that they are finding the school gossip difficult to handle, parents may need to see it for the cry for help it really is (see Chapter 8 for strategies).

'When I was 15 I really fancied a boy called Paul. All the girls fancied him — he was gorgeous and exciting. One night I met him at a party and I went outside into the garden with him. It was magical, one thing led to another and I thought we "made love" — my first time — in the garden that night. All the girls were spitting jealous and I felt like a queen for a few days. Looking back, I overdid the showing off and boasting about Paul, but my triumph was short-lived because soon after my reputation was in tatters. It turns out that some of the boys in the party had gone upstairs and they watched our "live sex show". A boy called Kevin had figured out that we could be seen from an upstairs window and it was he who led the charge upstairs. Kevin was one of those annoying boys who never really fitted in properly. It was strange though, because after this incident everyone suddenly thought he was all that.

I still can't believe that I didn't notice the boys upstairs; they must have been very quiet. Of course the boys filmed it all and put it online, but thankfully you can't really make the images out. Still,

I'm horrified that there is a "sex tape" online with my name on it. I've never told my parents; hopefully they will never find out because it would kill my dad.

Soon after, the boys started to call me "easy-spread" and everywhere I went they threw packets of butter at me. They used to leave butter at my locker and on my chair in school. Looking back, I think most people — except me — were thrilled by the drama of it all. Once, when I was on the school bus, everyone just kept showering me with all these little packets of butter; for the whole journey home they threw the butter at me. They must have had a whole box of them. It was a nightmare.

When I look back I can see that I was quite flirtatious and while many of the boys fancied me, equally, lots of the girls were jealous of me. I understand now why the girls were willing to "take me down". At the time, I just thought "Why don't they like me?" But I was probably annoyingly gleeful and conceited about pulling Paul.

The boys were a different story — there was this horrible culture of "slut-shaming" in our school that most of the boys just ran with. You would think that in the 21st century we might be beyond that, but they weren't in my school. Paul came out of this looking like the great stud and his stock rose even further. Kevin emerged from it by becoming much more popular, while for me, my schooldays were totally ruined by one drunken, hormonally charged night. I'm not sure I have anything to take away from the experience — other than the bitter knowledge that teenagers can be very cruel and so it's important to be self-protective.'

Emma, 18

It is extraordinary to me how often I hear girls being described as 'sluts' or 'slags' both by other girls and by boys. Although feminism is apparently in its third wave – or even its fourth wave – we are still in the Victorian age when it comes to teenage girls being free to enjoy teenage kicks. Sadly, this issue doesn't seem to be about to change any time soon, and so teenage girls usually need to be more wary and more self-protective about their sexuality than teenage boys. Many would argue that this is the way nature intends it to be as it is usually the girl who suffers more emotional angst with an unwanted pregnancy. However, many more would argue that we have managed to overcome many of the difficulties that 'nature' has apparently intended for us – the epidural, anaesthetics and contraception spring to mind – and so perhaps one day we can look to a future where teenage girls and boys are equally free to enjoy their developing sexuality.

The hormonal changes that are involved in adolescence are charged enough, without adding in the heady feeling teenage girls can experience when they first realise that they are being lusted after. This feeling of sexual power can make the girl feel almost infallible for a moment – sadly, all too often these feelings of sexual charge are all too often stymied by experiences of degrading, everyday sexism. (I remember when I was 16 years old, feeling fantastic in my new purple summer dress and walking exuberantly over O'Connell Bridge in Dublin city. Suddenly my very-new-found confidence was completely shattered by a middle-aged trucker who chose to honk his horn and roar 'Ye little ride' out the window of his lorry. It seemed like the whole world was laughing and staring at me. I thought I was going to die with shame and all the joy and sunshine went out of the day.)

Highly charged sexual feelings in boys can quickly lead to feelings of powerlessness as it seems the girls hold the keys to the magic kingdom, and yet the girls, who are said to have the power, often feel bewildered and insecure about whatever sexual power they may have. Caution is the watchword here as teenagers need to learn to 'hasten slowly' as they begin to try to figure out their sexuality and their sexual preferences. The combination of heightened emotions and hormonal changes can make everything seem ultra-important – however, it is the role of the parents to attempt to bring some maturity, humour and perspective to these emotionally fraught situations.

Teens need guidance during these complicated moments so that they can retain a balanced view of their friendships – even through the storms and stresses of adolescence. One of the major differences between teenagers today and teenagers in previous years is that teenagers today often have over a thousand 'friends' on social media but no one to call when they feel insecure or upset. Since the day Facebook misappropriated the word 'friend', 'friendship' has become a different concept from what it was when many adults were young. While once upon a time, friendship required time, contribution, care and reciprocation, nowadays all that is really required is a casual 'like' here and there and we can be 'Facebook friends'. It has been very noticeable to me that for many of the teenagers I see, their so-called best friends are often heavy on emotion and drama but quite light on authentic solidarity.

One of the many challenges facing young people today is learning how to differentiate between their social media pals and their real-life pals. Many people can be great friends on social media and yet, in real life, they might not hit it off quite so much. This wider social network is probably here to stay and so it is helpful for parents to understand the complexities surrounding friendships among teenagers today. The teenagers I meet are well aware of the difference between social media 'friends' and real-life 'friends'; however, many parents are less sure of the difference. Many adults confine their 'social media friendships' to their real-life friends while teenagers are rampant in their desire to have lots of approval from the online world and so they promiscuously make friends with everybody they can. Yet, as Brené Brown tells us, 'Social media has given us this idea that we should all have a posse of friends when in reality, if we have one or two really good friends, we are lucky.'[11]

3

The bully and the crew
Lions, hyenas and antelopes

'Not everyone has been a bully or the victim of bullies, but everyone has seen bullying, and seeing it, has responded to it by joining in or objecting, by laughing or keeping silent, by feeling disgusted or feeling interested.'

Octavia E. Butler

Some of us are lions, some are antelopes, and more of us are cheerleading hyenas. Some people are gentle and unassuming, others are aggressive and domineering, and the rest are often just part of the crowd. The gentler souls don't have a strong need for power and prefer to stay under the radar, and the need for power is easily satisfied in these gentle 'antelopes'. Meanwhile, more assertive people – the lions – are motivated by a strong need for power and are often aggressive and driven to ensure that they come out on top of any situation. The hyenas tend to stay safe by being part of the critical mass and being agreeable to the lions.

If we live in a tolerant community that appreciates that we all bring something different to the party, then everyone can thrive in their own individual way. However, if we live in a community that is focused on winning and succeeding, then the gentle and uncompetitive types can be left feeling inadequate and weak and the powerful and aggressive types can feel superior and entitled.

The traditional view of bullies as thundering oafs who resort to physical intimidation as a clumsy way of getting their way has been debunked too many times to retain much credibility. Yes, there are some dangerously aggressive idiots who enjoy physically intimidating smaller people (think of the stereotypical nightclub bouncer); however, the smart, popular and sarcastic bully has a significantly more widespread and more destructive impact on people's lives today.

The typical bully is often a powerful personality who has fallen into bullying as a dysfunctional method of entertainment. This individual is often morally disengaged, popular and unable to handle the level of power that they have.

Many bullies or controlling 'friends' are motivated by a consuming need to gain control of the situation and driven by the need to ensure that the world bends to their will. These powerful personalities choose to bully when a person (often unknowingly) rattles their cage. They have little empathy for the target – indeed, they often dehumanise the target – and they view the target as little more than a source of power and entertainment.

The typical bully often doesn't have a very developed guilty conscience or social conscience to begin with and they also tend to have a low level of moral reasoning. As they have a strong need to dominate any given situation, they often hold a dismissive attitude towards rules and regulations. They often lack problem-solving skills – and so when someone lower in the pecking order annoys them, rather than dealing with the conflict calmly and reasonably, they viciously attack instead.

The bullying dynamic

The most important thing for targets and parents of targets to do is to understand the bullying dynamic. The target needs to understand the bully's motivations, weaknesses and strengths. If they can't in any way fathom what is going on, then it is imperative to seek some support from counselling or friends for them to better understand the situation.

If the parent can pass an accurate understanding of the bullying dynamic on to the target, this can have a long-term, lasting impact as, if they gain a more profound understanding of human nature, they will be much more likely to navigate themselves away from dangerous waters in the future. On the other hand, if the target doesn't understand what is happening then it can take a very long time, if ever, for the target to emerge from the situation with their ego intact. A lack of understanding of the dynamic also bodes ill for the future because if the target doesn't understand what happened they may get bullied again because they don't know what to watch out for.

The 'pure' bully

The 'pure' bully is often an aggressive and arrogant person who enjoys the heady feelings that power often brings. This socially savvy and smart individual is unlikely to suffer from low self-esteem – indeed they are usually very confident socially. They are at the top of the food chain and they occupy the dominant role in any given situation.

This character almost always has sidekicks who have instinctively figured out that it would be beneficial to them to become friends with this dominant person: 'pure bullies' are often popular even if they aren't particularly 'liked' – although their so-called popularity is based upon fear and caution. It is interesting that studies show that the 'pure bully' shows lower states of arousal than most other people – they keep a cool head and don't get emotionally strung-out if something extreme happens. This is one of the main reasons why they are able to go the extra mile when harassing others – they don't feel emotionally engaged, while more sensitive people find that the bullying may make them feel guilty, bad or sick inside.[12]

The smart, good-looking and popular bully is often narcissistic with a large but fragile ego. They suspect that they are great but then they quickly become defensive and angry if it is brought to their attention that they aren't, perhaps, as fabulous as they believe themselves to be. Indeed, very deep down in the dark recesses of their mind they may (however, not always) nurture dark feelings of inferiority and compensate for this by pretending to themselves and to everyone else that they are superior. It is a complex dynamic and one not easily understood, especially by children, and yet, once people are made aware of the exact dynamics at play, then the target can better figure out how to relate with the bullies so that they don't end up in the lion's den.

Amy was 15 years old when she first arrived in my office. A good-looking, frank girl, she was musical, a keen basketball player and the captain of the school debating team. She came from a successful family and was very motivated to succeed. Amy had an innate need to dominate, which I noticed almost from the first moment she arrived into my office as she began to discuss the art

---

on the walls and then seamlessly went into a long story about one of the pictures.

Amy was attending counselling because she had been identified as the key ringleader of a group of girls who had been relentlessly taunting a younger autistic boy called Ben. The taunting had been described by Amy and her pals as 'just a bit of fun' but it was causing Ben significant distress. Everywhere they saw him the girls repeatedly called out 'Hey Ben Ten!' This might sound benign the first or tenth time you hear it, but if you have difficulties understanding how to act in a social setting, and if it's from a very loud group of popular, giggling, good-looking girls, it can become embarrassing and unsettling.

When Amy and I first began to work together she vociferously argued that she was technically doing nothing wrong. Amy was bored and she enjoyed beating the system — and she believed she was technically in the right because there was nothing wrong with saying 'Hey Ben Ten'. Amy's distinct lack of empathy meant that she had no understanding of Ben's pain. Amy thought that any pain that Ben felt was irrelevant because the girls were technically in the right. In Amy's world, life was one big competition and she had to come out on top.

Amy had high self-esteem; she ranked herself highly and saw those beneath her as less important. She had poor moral reasoning and believed that people who weren't as successful as she was didn't deserve success as much as she did.

Multigenerational studies often show us that certain traits can be easily handed down, and Amy's mother, Deirdre, was also hyper-competitive. Deirdre had raised Amy to believe that their *family were special; they were outside the law and the ordinary rules didn't apply to them. Amy was taught to have no respect for authority and that respect for others was only earned if a person were to 'beat' you. According to Deirdre and Amy, everyone lived on a hierarchy of respect and whoever wasn't good at music, sports or academically lived beneath you on the social chain.*

We had a long road, but, with authenticity and a continuous battle of wits, eventually Amy learned some moral reasoning and empathic understanding. Over many sessions Amy and I explored and analysed in detail what it might be like to be Ben. Teaching Amy empathy and moral engagement took some time, but she eventually realised how she and her friends had devastated Ben's life. But all this effort was worth it as Amy became a kinder and more compassionate person who wasn't so keen to harass other gentler souls.

There is a certain type of 'pure bully' who is 'woefully deficient'[13] at having the moral reasoning or compassion to understand or care about how other people are feeling. Some neuroscientists argue that some bullies suffer from a neurological deficit – they have a malfunction in the brain that prevents them from either understanding or caring about the pain of others.[14] (Of course, parents of children who have been bullied can feel outraged that the neuroscientists' argument suggests that rather than stamping out bullying we should instead show the bullies the same compassion that the bullies can't themselves demonstrate.)

But then, on the other hand, there are other possible explanations for cruel behaviour, as it is not only bullies who behave with callous disregard for the feelings of others. Some perfectly ordinary people, with perfectly typical brains, are also capable of 'turning off' their moral engagement. Indeed, moral disengagement is one of the key reasons why people bully and why others stand by and allow bullying to take place (see Chapter 5).

Sixty years after it was published, William Golding's chilling novel *Lord of the Flies* still shows us just how a group of kids can dehumanise their target and turn off their moral engagement. These boys were alone on an island and so, in a bid to control their environment, they quickly created a pecking order with Ralph as the leader.

The tension between groupthink and individuality is powerfully portrayed by Golding as he charts the boys' descent into savagery. In this novel – perhaps the most horrifying text about bullying that exists – the natural human impulse to live peacefully and symbiotically together is in conflict with another natural human impulse – the desire to gain power over any given situation. Ultimately, Simon, a gentle but unusual boy, and the slightly overweight but intelligent Piggy are killed by the beasts within the hearts of the little boys on the island.

How to handle the 'pure bully'

This person needs to be handled cleverly and with plenty of consideration and forethought. Not easily moved towards compassion or kindness, the easiest way to reduce the bullying is to figure out what kicks the chief bully is getting from bullying your child. If you can figure out the motivation of the bullying then it is up to you to think about how your child can no longer be part of the fuel that feeds the bully.

Is it boredom? Is the bully entertained by your child's reaction? Is the bully leading the group to go further and further in an attempt to get a certain reaction from your child? When is it worse? When is it improved? Is it worse or better online? Most important, who are the upstanders in the vicinity? Who can help and who refuses to help? Your child needn't trouble those who refuse to help but generally there will be some people in any group who feel guilty about their role and it is these people the target needs to focus on if they are to move away from being a target (more in Chapter 5).

Bully or failed leader?

Some parents are aware that their children could become bullies if given a certain set of circumstances. These parents can, at every opportunity, point out the lasting qualities of good leadership while at the same time contrasting them with the destructive impact of bullying behaviour. This will begin to foster for the child an expectation and belief that leadership is the way to go.

Helping the power-hungry child

If your child is a bit power-mad, then it's important for parents to acknowledge that in certain circumstances their power-hungry child may mindlessly fall into bullying. These children especially need to be taught kindness, moral reasoning and compassion. With these traits they can go from being a potential bully to being a potentially great leader. A bully is often a badly formed leader, so if you worry that your child is beginning to use their attributes in a negative manner, then, with some effort and commitment, you can redirect them.

Modelling kindness, empathy, morality and compassion is the easiest way to teach your children these traits. When you do something kind be sure to tell your children all about it and explain why it was a good experience for everyone involved. Teach your potential leader compassion and understanding towards other people — be quick to spot the way that gentler people among us are often better able to bring the group together. Explain how every group needs a variety of personalities if it is to work; how we need the reflective ones, the cautious ones, the funny ones and the brave ones.

Admitting that your child might have some bullying tendencies can be a great gift the parent can give the child because, with a bit of nurturing, most potential bullies can easily be guided towards leadership instead.

Below are some points that can be used to emphasise the qualities of leadership with children.

- A good leader leads by example, while a bully dominates and intimidates others. It is easy for parents to point out when they lead the family by example and when they fall by the wayside and use more bullying tactics.

- A leader is honest and shares information with everyone, while bullies tend to use information as a source of power.

- Leaders aren't threatened by other people's opinions – indeed, they welcome intelligent input into the situation, while bullies prefer to surround themselves with 'yes-men' and can't bear dissent.

- Leaders understand the different individuals in the group and they encourage each person according to their abilities, while bullies tend to have low expectations of everyone.

- Leaders have emotional intelligence and show good interpersonal skills so they can relate with others effectively. Bullies tend to be emotionally immature with a childishly competitive attitude towards the rest of the human race.

If your child is competitive, do the world a favour and teach them how to be a good sport. Competition can be very helpful in a general sense, but good sportsmanship is an essential component of an ethical competitor. Good sportsmanship teaches a person to treat people with compassion, empathy and dignity. The good news is that these traits will help them in all aspects of life, far beyond the local community games.

But it's not enough to recite the obligatory comments about 'being a good loser'. Instead, parents need to discuss what good sportsmanship means and how it impacts on the world. This means no cheating, no slagging off the competition and always being kind and respectful to anyone who loses. Both winning and losing a competition are golden teachable moments where parents need to step in and show children how to handle failure as well as how to handle success with dignity and empathy.

Examine notorious poor losers in professional sports and use this opportunity to point out how needless and nasty this behaviour is. Go on YouTube with your kids and look at old clips of McEnroe disputing match points at Wimbledon, Zola Budd apparently tripping Mary Decker, Arsène Wenger refusing to shake hands with the opposition and South Korean boxer Byun Jung-il crying his eyes out when he was fairly penalised for head-butting his opponent at the 1988 Seoul Olympics.

Discuss these incidents with them and compare them with contrasting stories of heroism and sportsmanship. Show them inspiring stories of people who had grace under pressure such as snooker and tennis players who, at a crucial point in the match, admitted that they had made a foul when no one had noticed, or Tana Umaga, the New Zealand rugby player who sacrificed his attacking position to put his opponent Colin Charvis in the recovery position. The famous football match on Christmas Day 1914 between British and German soldiers is another inspiring example that can eloquently teach children how grace matters more than beating your opponents.

If they don't manage to behave appropriately when they feel stressed, teach your child to admit that they're as fallible as the rest of us. As the spoken word artist Kate Tempest advises us: 'If you've been an arsehole today, acknowledge it. Try not to be one tomorrow.'

The victim-bully

The old saying 'hurt people hurt people' perfectly explains the genesis of the 'victim-bully', also known as the 'bully-victim'. Some people – 'victim-bullies' – experience the worst of both worlds: they experience bullying and then they become bullies. Studies show that this type of person often shows a higher degree of arousal than other people in certain situations and so they can tend to over-react in a stressful situation. It is interesting that in this context this type of person is the complete opposite of the 'pure bully'; the pure bully isn't easily moved to emotion and can be numb to other people's pain, while the victim-bully tends to over-react to emotional distress. Often described as highly strung with a heightened sensitivity to being overlooked or going unrewarded, the victim-bully can be ultra-sensitive to themselves but too self-absorbed to be sensitive to others. They are quick to anger and they haven't yet learned how to be a non-victim without lashing out, and so they can be hard work to be around.

'I was a bully when I was a kid. It happened accidentally, really. I was a strange-looking kid — ginger, freckles, really skinny and I had an unfortunate overbite — of course I wasn't as strange-looking as I believed I was, but I wasn't conventional-looking anyway. My parents really worshipped good-looking people — they were glamorous themselves and they put all their efforts into my sister who was gorgeous while I was ignored and dismissed. I had a cousin who was also a redhead and we were treated like the freak throwbacks of the family. I hate to admit it but the visceral hatred I had for strange-looking kids in my life was way over the top. I picked on anyone who looked different. Looking back, I was picking on them so that no one would notice my own physical differences, but it's no excuse really.

We made some kids' lives hell — I say "we", but really it was all led by me. We called one girl in my class "the Freak" — her real name was Sinéad — and we made her life hell. We texted her nasty messages, we publicly taunted her on social media and we constantly sent her images of ugly-looking people to offer them as members of her "Freak Club" which we set up online. It was all incredibly nasty but we thought we were hilarious at the time. In the end, her parents pulled her out of the school. I met Sinéad just recently and she was really cool looking and seemed very confident. She was fine with me and didn't say anything about those years when we wrecked her life. I'm ashamed of how I behaved as a teenager. The only excuse I can offer is that I was a dreadfully unhappy and insecure kid at the time.'

Rebecca, 23

The victim-bully is quite the opposite of the pure bully. They *do* have low self-esteem, they often have problems fitting in and may 'fail' some of the narrow-minded social boundaries that teenagers set among themselves. They may not be particularly bright or particularly good-looking or particularly 'anything' that makes them cool in teen-world. However, they may stand out in some negative way and have come to the conclusion that this is why they were bullied and this is how the world works. Sadly, this is why they feel justified for their behaviour as they then reflect back what they receive.

The victim-bully is often given to self-pity as they tend to be completely self-absorbed and tend to only understand things from their own point of view. In a way, their sense of being a victim becomes a crutch and a reason to justify future cruel behaviour. A negative cycle can begin where the victim-bully feels filled with self-pity, justification and self-absorption rather than worrying about the damage that they are causing the target. The natural empathy they might have once had can be washed away in a sea of narcissism and self-pity. They have decided that lashing out because you are angry is a valid excuse and they often believe that their hurt is more important than others'.

Many victim-bullies jump over the line from assertiveness to bullying when they finally face down their bully and they realise it feels good in the moment. When an assertive response turns out well, the rush of power can easily go to their head. The potential victim-bully suddenly realises that they can control a situation and, feeling empowered by this rush of adrenalin, they soon turn on others who are weaker than themselves. Because they are highly emotional anyway, victim-bullies particularly enjoy the heightened feelings of power and control when they begin bullying others.

They are often less concerned about being first in the competition of popularity, but instead are desperately compelled to ensure they aren't last.

Victim-bullies usually hold a Machiavellian view of life, with a lack of faith in human nature; as a consequence of their experience when they were bullied, they have become cynical, hardened and embittered. The often cruelly humorous nature of bullying can give them a sense of glee when they target other people as they are thrilled that they aren't being victimised and they become determined to ensure that the victim fares even worse than they did – again, in a bitter bid to ensure that they aren't the least popular in the group.

The difference between 'pure bullies' and 'victim-bullies' is significant in that pure bullies are often insensitive and don't seem to know any better, while victim-bullies know exactly the damage they are causing and, perhaps because of their own dark personal experiences, are motivated to continue to cause the target pain and anguish.

What to do if your child is targeted by a 'victim-bully'

It is imperative that the child begins to learn about the complex motivations of the victim-bully. If your child can understand that the hurt and anger that the victim-bully is showing reveals more about the victim-bully than themselves, then they can begin to gain perspective on the situation and realise that it isn't their fault.

The victim-bully can be more easily cowed by a show of strength than the less emotional 'pure bully'. If your child can build up a network of upstanders who are willing to step up for them, the victim-bully will very quickly retreat and look for easier prey.

> The target should ask the victim-bully to repeat their bitchy comments — as if they hadn't heard them. The victim-bully is often not quite strong enough to say these comments again. The victim-bully is easily intimidated.

The bully's crew

Most bullies need the approval of the group if they are to continue bullying; a few sidekicks the bully can rely on to laugh at their cruel jokes and to give them the critical mass that is needed for the bully to become a strong force. The crew are often mostly insecure 'yes-men', usually living on their wits as they realise their social status relies solely on staying on the right side of the bully. The individuals in the group may not have the charisma or the good looks that the bully has, but instead they have the strategic intelligence to know how to align themselves with the most powerful person in the group.

Rosalind Wiseman's book *Queen Bees and Wannabes*[15] inspired the 2004 hit movie *Mean Girls*. Wiseman's book shows us that life can be very intense and dramatic in 'Girl World' and teenagers' lives are made and destroyed on the emotional rollercoaster of who's in, who's out, who's cool, who's not. Many people presume that this social hierarchy is mostly for girls and that boys prefer to just 'fight any difficulties out'. However, in my work I have found that boys, just as much as girls, are very concerned with their social position within the group and can feel just as dejected and isolated if they're ignored on social media or not invited to an important social event 'irl'.

In her book, Wiseman categorises everybody's roles and shows us how a group of bullies is usually a sophisticated group with a strict hierarchy that doesn't allow for non-conformity. Not only does Wiseman describe the role of the bully and the sidekick but the roles of the banker, the torn bystander, the pleaser, the wannabe and the floater are also detailed in her book. Although Wiseman chose to separate the sexes and wrote a different book for boys, *Ringleaders and Sidekicks*, the conclusions and analyses are similar.

The popular 'Queen Bee' or 'Ringleader' might denigrate a quieter, less popular kid at every opportunity simply because they are bored and enjoy the heady feeling of power they get when they make jokes at the quiet kid's expense. The 'lieutenant' (the sidekick) is always on hand with funny but cruel remarks to back up the ringleader. The 'banker' hoards information like gold and uses the information to place themselves in a strategically powerful position in the group. This person often acts as the self-important messenger between groups and feels satisfied that by being 'in the know' they will always have a relatively important position. The 'pleaser' and the 'wannabe' ruthlessly follow the leader and the sidekick hoping one day to gain more status and approval from the group (and sometimes they do), while the 'torn bystanders' tend to wring their hands in despair at any bad behaviour but are too fearful to act upon their moral conscience. Interestingly, it is the 'torn bystander' who is often more complicit in the drama than oblivious bystanders as they understand more than others what's going on and they can often more easily empathise with the target's pain. Fear of becoming a target and fear of becoming unpopular usually ensures that the torn bystanders keep quiet (often against their better judgement).

The 'floater' in Wiseman's book is the person who floats from group to group without becoming embroiled in the politics of any given group. I was a floater in my secondary school and it was often a lonely and insecure position, yet with my peculiar nature, it was my only option. I was so horrified by the groupthink that characterised the groups in the school I just couldn't join in any of the cliques – indeed I felt nervous and hassled if any group tried to own me. I was also a floater in my primary school but the vibe in the primary school wasn't nearly as competitive or insecure as the secondary school and so I didn't feel remotely anxious in my primary school.

The 'floater' usually retains their own personality, happy to be classified as slightly weird or different as they believe it is a worthwhile sacrifice to make in exchange for freedom and independence. But this person can easily move from being a 'floater' to a 'loner' to a 'freak' and so it is a very insecure position – especially these days as the cult of personality has become ever more popular and being a loner is often viewed with suspicion and hostility.

Nurturing the nature: good and evil

One ordinary working day in October 2005, the neuroscientist James Fallon was sifting through thousands of PET scans to find anatomical patterns in the brain that correlated with psychopathic tendencies in the real world. 'I was looking at many scans, scans of murderers mixed in with schizophrenics, depressives and other, normal brains,' he said. 'Out of serendipity, I was also doing a study on Alzheimer's, and as part of that, had brain scans from me and everyone in my family right on my desk.'[16]

We can only imagine Fallon's shock when he realised that one of the brain scans from his family correlated with the brain scan of a psychopath. 'I got to the bottom of the stack, and saw this scan that was obviously pathological.' This brain scan showed low activity in certain areas of the frontal and temporal lobes linked to empathy, morality and self-control, and indicated psychopathic tendencies in this person's brain. Fallon's first response was to check the PET machine for an error (it was working perfectly fine) and then decided he needed to know who it was in his family who had the brain of a psychopath. His initial shock must have turned to horror when he looked up the code and it was revealed that the psychopathic brain pictured in the scan was his own.

Fallon was intrigued by this, as he says, 'I've never killed anybody, or raped anyone. So the first thing I thought was that maybe my hypothesis was wrong, and that these brain areas are not reflective of psychopathy or murderous behaviour.' Consequently, Fallon underwent a series of genetic tests and he found out that he had genes that were linked with aggressive behaviour. Eventually, Fallon, having done extensive research into neurological and behavioural psychopathy, decided that he was indeed a psychopath – just a nice version of one.

Fallon calls himself a 'pro-social psychopath'; he has difficulty feeling true empathy for others, but as a result of his good upbringing and his relatively positive environment, Fallon keeps his behaviour within socially acceptable bounds. Many of us would bury the brain scan and not tell a soul, but Fallon (perhaps as a consequence of his psychopathic tendencies) was bolder than that and decided to go public with his information. He has since published a book about this event, *The Psychopath Inside: A Neuroscientist's Personal Journey into the Dark Side of the Brain*, and has done TED talks on the subject.

Fallon, once a self-proclaimed geneticist, has come to the conclusion that the nurturing of his nature has played a significant role in how he has turned out. 'I was loved, and that protected me,' he says of his family upbringing. Fallon was desperately wanted by his parents as he arrived after a series of miscarriages and he believes the extra love and attention he received from his parents was what saved him from travelling down a more dysfunctional path. Although he was raised in a loving family, Fallon still showed some other tell-tale signs as he was growing up, such as panic attacks, obsessive-compulsive tendencies and social anxieties. 'Looking at my genetics, I had [a] lethal combination, but I just had the happiest childhood growing up,' he said. 'There were dark periods I went through, but [my parents] didn't bring me to a psychiatrist, but they told my sisters and teachers to watch out for me,' he said. 'My mother instinctively knew there was a problem.'[17]

A professor of psychiatry and human behaviour, Fallon's personality certainly appears to be distinctly cold, as can be seen when he told ABC News.com, 'When somebody gets mad at me, I never show it – they can't read it on my face. I never get even immediately, but four years down the road, I get them with revenge.'

Interestingly, there were seven alleged murderers in Fallon's family ancestry. Fallon himself notes that just like other psychopaths he is especially motivated by power and manipulating others. He also admits that he is aggressive, he lacks empathy and he is a risk-taker. Fortunately, not all psychopaths kill; some, like Fallon, exhibit different types of psychopathic behaviour. 'I'm obnoxiously competitive. I won't let my grandchildren win games. I'm kind of an asshole, and I do jerky things that piss people off,' he says. 'But while I'm aggressive, my aggression is sublimated. I'd rather beat someone in an argument than beat them up.'

Before Fallon made his astonishing discovery, he was very much on the side of nature in the nature versus nurture debate. As he says, 'I was the poster boy for genes causing everything. But I had to eat crow and say I was wrong.' According to Fallon, a person born with psychopathic tendencies is a loaded gun, but not necessarily a death sentence, because it is only within a certain environment that the potential psychopath will be pushed over the edge to become a psychopathic killer. A lot of people have the symptoms – shrewd, selfish, cold and calculating – but they never get the full package. As Fallon says, 'I wouldn't want to marry me. I am a pain in the ass and competitive. I can be so manipulative and I am always on the make, but I am not going to kill anyone or rape anyone.'

Is it a dangerous over-simplification to label some people as intrinsically 'good' and others as intrinsically 'evil'? Do 'bad' people commit crimes and, since they are innately 'bad', should we lock them up and throw away the key? The case of James Fallon and recent developments in neuroscience suggest that some people are born with a larger or smaller predisposition to be kind or unkind. Perhaps we should sympathise with 'bad' people as nature has given them a difficult and unlikeable trait. Should we view 'good people' as genetically lucky and 'bad people' as genetically unlucky?

Fortunately – or unfortunately as the case may be – human nature is much more complex than this. Good and evil are flexible concepts, as one person's version of 'good' is another person's 'weak'. In addition, most – but not all – 'evil' behaviour comes about as a consequence of social learning or suffering an abusive childhood. What's more, some 'evil' people can be rehabilitated and eventually come good, displaying qualities such as empathy and kindness.

Many experts believe that we are still swinging off the trees in terms of our knowledge of the intricacies of human morality. We have no idea really about why some people have such a large capacity to be good on the one hand and then gleefully sadistic on the other. This is why we need to be mindful that it is much more powerful and helpful to try to understand the motivation and the perspective of the bullying situation so that we can figure out how bullies can be guided to a better way of behaving, how the bystanders can be moved to act responsibly and how the target can learn to avoid the evil eye of the bully.

Many psychologists and neuroscientists believe that it is how we 'nurture the nature' that impacts more than any other aspect of raising children to be kind and engaged adults. And so our role as parents is to nurture potential bullies to be fair leaders, encourage the bystanders to act as upstanders instead and support potential targets so that they learn how to respond appropriately as soon as they are targeted.

4

The target

Tall poppies, provocative victims and gentle souls

'No one can make you feel inferior without your consent.'

Eleanor Roosevelt

It's a tragic reality that there have been so many suicides attributed to bullying that we now have a word to describe it: bullycide. There are targets all over the world at this very minute contemplating whether their existence on this earth is worth it, whether they can bear any more of the cruelty or if they should just give up and end it all. More than anything, the aim of this book is to help the targets of bullying (both potential and current); to help them learn how to handle the bullies, how to avoid the bullies, how to build a circle of support, how to complain effectively and, most of all, how to stand their sacred ground. However, if we are to significantly reduce the impact of bullying, the targets of bullying need not only to gain further insight into the personalities of the bullies, the bystanders, the upstanders and the adults in charge, but they also need to gain a deeper emotional insight into themselves as they learn to figure out the impact of their thoughts, feelings and behaviour.

Many bullies are self-absorbed and if we tell a bully 'not to bully' it is unlikely that they will suddenly slap their forehead, see the light and become as gentle as a lamb. It is more likely that they will feel their cage has been rattled and, with an instinctive and powerful need to regain control, they will up the ante instead. And so the parents of the child who is being bullied need to help their targeted child to rise above and away from the malevolent bullies instead.

For a target of bullying to move from feeling entirely powerless to feeling that they can bring about change in their world will often be a slow, painstaking process. The parent will need to help their child to dig deep to find the power that lies within them. The primary aim for a target should be to create a situation where it is no longer so easy to bully them – this can be as a result of their own actions or because of the bystanders or the authorities in charge. If the target can create a situation where it is a hassle to the bully to bully them then, depending on the environment, the bully will either search for easier prey or find something more positive to do.

The impact of bullying

Being bullied feels like being trapped, mute, silenced by forces beyond your control and absolutely riddled with feelings of shame. Elaine, a 19-year-old girl, describes it eloquently:

> Profoundly ashamed, you feel completely powerless, isolated and alone in a world filled with people who seem to be able to manage better than you can. You feel like you don't matter. Perhaps the worst bit of it is feeling as if your isolation is contagious as often former friends drop you and act as if they will catch 'loser' from you.

Here are some common traits and outcomes that are often experienced by the victims in a bullying situation.

- Targets often feel defeated by the bullying and feel as if they are all alone in the world with no one to turn to. They may begin to think that the whole world is against them and they just have to learn to accept this.

- If it's been happening over a period of time, the target begins to feel that the bullying is their fault and that they deserve the bullying.

- Targets can feel they are stuck with the bullying, that it is an inevitable consequence for being the way they are – they can even feel guilty for wanting the bullying to stop.

- Targets feel like they are 'wrong' on some level; that they don't fit in for some hidden reason.

- Because targets feel that they are 'wrong', they often try to change their deepest self.

- In an attempt to cope with deep feelings of inadequacy and tension, targets often become self-destructive and become more at risk of mental health issues.

- Some targets become very self-deprecating and self-critical; they try to stay onside with the bullies by turning against themselves. For example, they might become a class clown.

- Some targets are a victim of 'tall poppy syndrome' and they begin to hide their talents in a bid to assuage the bullies.

- If the teachers don't help to stop the bullying or, worse, the teachers are bullies, the target can feel more profoundly inadequate and disliked, threatened, confused, stressed and panicky.

- Some targets who have an outwardly defining characteristic – e.g. a wheelchair – feel that their true self is ignored.

- The target might feel compelled to hide their true self such as their sexual orientation or economic circumstance as they believe that this is the sole reason for the bullying.[18]

Why are some people targeted?

Many people feel that they have been bullied so often that they must have a sign on their head saying 'Bully Me' – and, I hate to say it, but they almost do. Bullies can pick out their prey in an instinctive manner; they are often highly attuned to who is the easiest prey, what is the pecking order in any social situation and they are usually spurred on by their survival instinct and their need for power.

Child sexual predators who were interviewed while they were in prison were asked what sort of children they tended to target. The response they gave was shocking – it wasn't the cute kids that they especially chose, nor was it the sexually precocious kids. Rather, the paedophiles said that they chose the kids who don't tell. Similarly, it is said that the serial killer Ted Bundy could pick out his prey simply by the way they walked down the street. And so it is that bullies instinctively choose the people who will endure the bullying without fighting back. The instinct to fight back is almost automatic – some of us instinctively fight back when we are attacked while others shy away from the conflict. Those who instinctively fight back are less likely to endure protracted bullying, as the bullies prefer to overpower easier prey. If your body language is gentle, timid or subservient, bullies are more likely to consider you easy prey: indeed, if you are stoical, non-combative and quiet, if you tend to be a little bit different and if you live in a competitive atmosphere, then you are possibly already on some bully's radar somewhere.

To ensure your children never get bullied, here's an easy and foolproof plan; all you need to do is teach your children the following:

- **Stay under the radar.** Never get noticed for being good, bad or indifferent.

- **Be extroverted.** Whether that comes naturally or not (but not too extroverted).

- **Seek out the stronger characters.** Teach your kids to ingratiate themselves into any group.

- **Be immediately aggressive.** They must be ready to fight at any hint of attack.

- **Act as the sidekick.** Tell them to become the yes-man, suppressing values in a bid to conform with the group.

- **Be funny and self-deprecating.** They should be ready to be part of the joke.

- **Value popularity over values or beliefs.** Teach them to be liked by everyone – even by people they don't actually like themselves.

- **Be sly.** Explain how they should always be on high alert for weaker people acting differently so that they can point this idiosyncratic behaviour out to the strongest, most powerful members of the group

Hmmm, it's not all that great is it? In fact, it's kind of distasteful. The corollary of this is that the traits below show us the type of person who is much more likely to be bullied:

- **Being different.** Anyone who dares to be different; anyone who is brave enough to put their head over the parapet and tries to actually do something significant is in danger of being bullied. Bullies target anyone who is different. It doesn't really matter whether the difference is good or bad; just being different is enough.

- **Being nice and gentle.** Being different isn't the only reason – although it is certainly the most likely reason – that people are bullied. Some people are targeted by bullies because they are gentle souls – nature's pacifists for whom physical violence is distasteful. Although these people are rarely a threat, they are easy prey for someone who is seeking a short, sharp shock of superiority.

- **Not being a leader.** In the jungle, the lion doesn't go for another lion but for easier prey such as the antelope. Likewise, bullies focus on the people who are perceived as 'lower' on the social hierarchy because it's easier. If you are well-liked or if you have natural leadership or highly developed social skills, bullies will keep their distance from you as they will instinctively feel that there are other targets out there who would be much easier to bully.

- **Being stoical.** Some people can quietly endure pain for much longer than others. Bullies prefer to target this type of person as they will be unlikely to fight back and they are also less likely to complain about their experiences. Instead they bravely and quietly endure their lives of quiet desperation, hoping that the bullies will one day move on.

- **Being insecure.** People who are insecure are often easy targets for bullies as they are much less likely to assert themselves adequately and so the bullies will get away with it.

So, to recap, people who are targeted by bullies are often different, they are often gentle and stoical and some of them have no particular desire to be in the limelight. Added to this they are often insecure about themselves – perhaps as a consequence of their other traits in our dog-eat-dog world – and it is this combination that makes them more likely to be bullied. In striking contrast, as we saw in Chapter 3, bullies are often arrogant, hyper-competitive, quick to anger, incompetent at handling conflict and power-crazy. Tragically, the targets are often much kinder people than the bullies; yet another manifestation of Mother Nature's diabolical rules of the universe.

The bestselling author Stephen King's first novel, *Carrie*, was made into a horrifying movie that starkly portrays the misery of being a misfit in a bullying environment. In this excerpt, King writes about a girl called Dodie who he knew in high school. Dodie was a partial inspiration for his fictitious account of Carrie, who was bullied to a horrifying climax. Dodie and her brother Bill would wear the same clothes every day to school, and were subjected to vicious bullying because of this.

> *The other girls made fun of her; at first behind her back and then to her face. Teasing became taunting. The boys weren't a part of it. We had Bill to take care of. Yes, I helped. Not a whole lot, but ... I was there. Dodie had it worse, I think. The girls didn't just laugh at Dodie. They hated her, too. Dodie was everything they were afraid of.*
>
> *After Christmas vacation of our sophomore year, Dodie came back to school resplendent. The dowdy old black*

skirt had been replaced by a cranberry colored one that stopped at her knees, instead of halfway down her shins. The tatty knee socks had been replaced by nylon stockings which looked pretty good because she had finally shaved the luxuriant mat of black hair off her legs. The ancient sleeveless blouse had given way to a soft wool sweater. Dodie was a girl transformed and you could see by her face that she knew it.

... It doesn't matter because mere clothes change nothing. The teasing that day was worse than ever. Her peers had no intention of letting her out of the box they'd put her in. She was punished for even trying to break free.

... I saw her smile fade, saw the light in her eyes first dim, and then go out. By the end of the day she was the girl she'd been before Christmas vacation – a doe-faced, freckle-cheeked wraith, scurrying through the halls with her eyes down and her books clasped to her chest.

Someone made a break for the fence and had to be knocked back down. That was all. Once the escape was foiled and the entire company of prisoners was accounted for, life could go back to normal.

... Dodie was dead by the time I started writing Carrie.[19]

Sadly, perhaps inevitably, Dodie died by suicide.

Many of us have known a Dodie – indeed, a visceral memory of a child just like Dodie during my own childhood is one of the many reasons why I felt compelled to write this book.

Perhaps the saddest aspect of this tale is when Dodie arrived back to school after Christmas all dressed up and ready to begin her new life. The bullies wouldn't let her break the social order and so of course the bullies broke her again. There is an important lesson to be learned here – parents often buy their kids the latest iPhone or Nike trainers or whatever in a desperate but doomed bid to improve their child's social status, but other kids can see through these ploys like a pane of glass. If you really want to improve your child's social standing in a difficult environment, you will have to accept that this will not be an overnight job. It may indeed include buying the latest iPhone or Nike trainers, but there will be many false starts, many falls and many lessons learned so, in this context, you and your child need to prepare yourselves for the long game.

The real question is whether Dodie could have done anything to escape the abuse. Her parents were no help and they couldn't teach her how to adjust to social norms. Although some people, like Stephen King, were sympathetic, Dodie didn't have any wise counsellor to advise her to head towards the kinder and more compassionate children in the school. Sadly, Dodie misguidedly thought that the new outfit would be enough, but a longer and more sustained effort was required to emerge triumphant in this situation. The survival instinct of humans is designed so that neediness arouses fear and caution within us.[20] In the world of bullies, cool kids, cliques and freaks, many kids attempt to stay within spitting distance of the popular kids – the closer they get to the unpopular kids, the closer they get to being bullied. So sympathetic kids – torn bystanders – such as Stephen King himself didn't get close to Dodie or her brother for fear of contamination of their own social status.

The bullies couldn't forgive Dodie for thinking a new look would so easily penetrate their barriers to entry. They knew where she was from and they weren't so easily fooled by a new outfit. Dodie's bullies kept control of the situation by showing that they were powerful – they instinctively knew they would have appeared weak and foolish by allowing her pass muster so easily.

Learning from Dodie's story

If your child is socially ostracised by the group then it will take a significant level of time and commitment to change the situation. Your child will have to understand the personalities of everyone involved, including the adults, and they will also need to gain a deeper understanding of their place in society. Thinking that one dramatic change will be enough to stop the bullies is hopelessly naive — what is needed is a long-term plan of challenging and changing the target's reactions to the bullying, the school environment's acceptance of the bullying, and the bystanders' complicit inaction when the bullying occurs.

The target needs to learn what's valued in the group and what is ridiculed; what annoys the group and what angers the group; what is considered 'cool' and what is 'uncool' so as to have a better understanding of the dynamic at play. Involved parents may need to teach their children these social intricacies if the child is missing them.

The target needs to learn how to anticipate dangerous situations and head them off at the pass, e.g. it might be a good idea to avoid public toilets and other vulnerable areas when the bullying is at a height.

The good news is that all this concerted effort from both the parents and the child will ensure that your child learns many social skills and this will mean that your child is a lot less likely to be targeted again in the future.

Tall poppy syndrome

For many children, the distribution of power in the group is perceived as a zero-sum game (i.e. if the total gains of the participants are added up and the total losses are subtracted, they will come to zero). And so, in this world, one person's gain of power is exactly balanced and equal to another's loss of power.

In certain groups, there is only a limited amount of prestige available and for someone to rise in status, another must fall. It is for this reason that many people feel unsettled by the successful performance of the high achiever – they feel that the tall poppy's gain is automatically going to result in some loss of status for them. So potential bullies are quick to humiliate or sabotage the high achiever so as to supplant them in the group hierarchy.

The herd instinct prefers everyone to stick together, to stay the same and to maintain the status quo – no matter how unhappy it is. Similarly, when a group of crabs are placed in a bucket and one attempts to crawl out, the other crabs grab at the escapee, perhaps in an attempt to jump on the back of their success. But it doesn't work, and the crab then falls back into the bucket.

It is often very difficult for targets of envy – the tall poppies – to handle the begrudgery and resentment that arises in others. People who are dissatisfied with their lives find it gratifying to tell more outwardly impressive people that they're not that great. These 'haters' often hide behind humour as a means to ridicule and disparage people's success; and, sadly, the internet has given these bitter and cynical types an outsized platform to freely make their catty remarks.

The best way to deal with tall poppy syndrome is to analyse the situation with the child so that the child understands the dynamics at play. Support from the family can be nurturing at this insecure time, and the 'tall poppy' might also gain some profound comfort from the arts or from stories about celebrities who didn't fit in as children but who went on to achieve great success as adults (see Chapter 9). In addition, other children who are equally successful or impressive can give great succour and encouragement to the tall poppy. If a child is forced to always be in the company of other children who aren't similar to them then they can feel isolated and alone. However, if the parent can ensure that their child meets others who are like them in some way then it is more likely that the child will feel stronger and more positive about their own identity.

When your child has a high need to 'fit in'

The American psychologist William Glasser believed that we are all, at heart, in search of connection. Some people have a particularly high need to fit in, to have a sense of belonging and to be a part of the group, while others don't. Arguing with your child that they shouldn't feel the need to fit in can often miss the point; some people benefit more than others from a sense of belonging and it is not necessarily a 'lack' in the child.

If your child has a noticeably high need to belong then it would be very helpful if you can accept this as part of their personality and find a few groups for them to satisfy their need for belonging (one group isn't enough for this type of person because if this group falls apart then they will need another group to fall back on).

Your child might suit the local football club, the scouts or a drama group; it really doesn't matter, so long as the group is a healthily functioning group rather than a random group of friends without any particular focus. This is not to say that your child shouldn't pick their own group of mates — people with a high need to belong usually have a need for a group of their own pals — but it is up to the parents to ensure that one group of friends isn't their sole source of kinship so that these kids aren't vulnerable to becoming needy and desperate to fit in.

Just as bullies are on a continuum from 'pure bullies' to 'bystanders', so are targets on a continuum from 'passive targets' to 'provocative targets'. In an archetypal bullying environment, certain types of people can inadvertently invite bullies to target them. The more we can identify the subtleties in our children's behaviour and the challenges of the environment (see Chapter 6), the more we can identify the most effective and helpful action for the future.

The passive target

This person generally possesses certain traits that provoke the bully into believing they are easy prey. They may have low self-esteem and they often feel completely overwhelmed when they attract the negative attention of a bully. They are simply too gentle for an aggressive environment and the parents of these gentle souls need to be ultra-sensitive as to whether their school environment suits them, because some children wilt in a competitive, dog-eat-dog environment.

The passive target might have some close friends but in certain environments their friends – who might be gentle too – might be afraid to befriend them as they realise that it is socially dangerous to be friendly with them. A more assertive person wouldn't allow their friends to treat them in this way but a passive person will allow their friends to mistreat them.

The more extreme passive target may prefer to just stay home and will willingly miss out on some fun activities rather than be out in the rough, tough world. They may make narrow choices as a direct result of their logical and rational fear and distaste for the competitive environment. Sometimes this sweet, sensitive, naive type of person has never learned to protect their sensitive nature from those who are harsher or rougher. They might be described as 'hopelessly naive' or 'lacking self-protection'. Some of them are socially or physically awkward, while others are simply nice, gentle quiet people.

Building a circle of support for the passive target

✓ **Find their element.** This type of person needs to be helped to find a safe place where the people roll in a gentler and more peaceful manner. It's very important that their parents wholly accept their mild and passive nature and refrain from urging them to 'toughen up'. A gentle and quiet strength is a more helpful trait to nurture in this person. Parents need to help their children to seek out and attend clubs that are appreciative and supportive of their personality.

✓ **Respect your passive child's utterances.** A passive child who is told, 'You've no reason to be upset,' or 'Don't be sad' feels undermined by their parent. Dismissing their feelings prevents the child from having the opportunity to become self-aware, and without self-awareness it is very hard to learn to self-regulate. If the parent habitually overrides the child's emotions then a bully will find it easier to override the child's feelings. There are no good or bad emotions; they are just emotions. Children need to be taught to trust their feelings and to honour them. It is more helpful if parents validate their children's feelings without adding anything.

✓ **Help them practise being assertive.** When the family is at home, parents can provide their gentle children with the opportunity to practise saying 'no' and to see that a simple 'no' can be effective. Parents need to teach children to trust their emotions so that they can learn their emotional boundaries, so that when the day comes when they need to say 'no' they can say 'no' with the expectation that they will be listened to. This helps them to have the courage of their convictions when they need it.

✓ **Help them practise finding their 'strong voice'.** Your strong voice is in a lower tone than your ordinary voice. Parents can teach children to practise lowering their voice when they are threatened — they can role-play with their family and friends — so that they can practise how to stand their ground.

✓ **Teach them to respond quickly to an attack.** This is often the hardest thing to teach the passive target as their instinctive reaction to an attack is anything but fight — they would much rather flee, freeze or desperately try to appease the attacker. This type of person is unlikely to suddenly learn to be highly assertive; however, they can learn certain gestures that can be effective, e.g. when the bully arrives into their space the passive target might learn to immediately walk away — thereby showing that they will not hang around to be insulted. Speed of response matters in this situation — if they are to reduce the bullying, the bully needs to feel that it is a hassle to bully the passive target.

✓ **Help them to maintain old friendships.** The parents can ensure this happens by noticing which of their friends are particularly supportive and ensure that these friends remain in their world — as Polonius advised Hamlet, 'Those friends thou hast, and their adoption tried, Grapple them unto thy soul with hoops of steel'. The parent might need to be proactive here as this gentle soul might not be the type to assertively ensure that a friendship remains alive if circumstances get in the way. If the parent is keeping an eye on this then it doesn't matter if the two friends go to different schools or have different hobbies — indeed, sometimes that's exactly what these kids need; supportive friends from different walks of life. The parents can ensure the circle of supportive friends around their passive child is kept active so that in times of stress old friends can be visited for some positive affirmation and validation.

✓ **Help them find their passion(s).** Passive targets often benefit from having a passion and this can also be nurtured by the parents. They might be mad about animals, so maybe they could have their own dog or be encouraged to volunteer at an animal shelter, or they might like drama, and so the parents could bring them to the theatre at every opportunity. It doesn't really matter what the passion is — and it doesn't matter if the passion is a passing whim — as long as the passive target gets the opportunity to forget about the rougher and more competitive side of life and escape to their comfort zone regularly.

✓ **Help them find other outside interests.** These kids need to be helped to belong to something else, something bigger than themselves. A political cause or a sports club can fit the bill in this context. Again, the passive target might need some extra encouragement to find this something else, but once found, they can keep it as another element of their circle of support and a reminder that they have worth.

✓ **Encourage them to appreciate nature.** Nature can bring great sustenance to the passive target. As Anne Frank said, 'The best remedy for those who are afraid, lonely or unhappy is to go outside, somewhere where they can be quite alone with the heavens, nature and God. Because only then does one feel that all is as it should be and that God wishes to see people happy, amidst the simple beauty of nature.' The passive target needs solace outside the furnace of the bullying; a reminder that the world is bigger than the bullies. Nature can be a good teacher for this person, a reminder that there is both kindness and cruelty in nature and, if we use some protective measures, we can weather most storms and wait for the sun to shine again. There are of course a million different ways for children to get in touch with nature, such as camping, hiking in the mountains or swimming in the sea or lakes.

When targets play the clown

The class clown often feels that they are teetering on the edge of being seriously bullied and so they turn to wildly clowning around to make people laugh in a bid to deflect a more serious situation arising. For example, they might laugh at their own obesity and accentuate it for a cheap laugh from their schoolmates. The clown often knows full well that everyone is laughing at them but they are too scared to allow the laughter to stop. The clown's bullying schoolmates are rarely content with a few laughs and they tend to egg them on to greater and greater feats of humiliation. The clown often plays to the gallery and pretends that it's all done in great jest, but they dishonour themselves, degrade themselves and they do serious damage to their self-esteem.

Helping the clown

- ✓ **Help them to harness their talent.** This person needs to harness the ability they have to make people laugh and channel it in another way. The bullies will become angry when the clown stops performing, but in the long term the clown needs to take some time to lie low as they begin to learn how to redirect their humour in a healthier manner.

- ✓ **Take the power back.** Clowns can take their ability to make people laugh but learn to ensure that they aren't focusing on all the things about themselves that are embarrassing. They need to take their power back and learn the difference between laughing at themselves and laughing at life. They need to learn to honour themselves and take their place in world.

✓ **Teach them to see the serious side.** Parents can help the clown by having quite serious conversations with them at every opportunity — even when the child continually acts the clown. The parents can laugh a little at the jokes the clown makes but then immediately return back to the serious conversation. The clown might resist this and it is the parents' job to fish out some serious stories from the news that might interest their child.

✓ **Encourage healthy comedy.** Parents can simultaneously work with their child's comedic personality by bringing them to comedy shows or showing them comedians on YouTube and pointing out the difference between laughing at yourself and laughing at the world.

The accidental target

This person, although not necessarily the Queen Bee or Mr Popularity, is usually ticking along happily and minding their own business when something unfortunate happens and they accidentally fall into the radar of the bullies. Sometimes what happens is innocuous enough, but if they are in a bullying environment and if the bullies are bored enough or feel threatened and insecure enough, they can seize upon the accidental target. Before the incident these targets are often ordinary members of the group, but suddenly they need to learn to dig deeper – right in the middle of a very traumatic experience.

'I was an ordinary boy with a few friends, neither madly popular nor particularly unpopular when one day, at the end of first year, I was happily getting changed after swimming and in the midst of all the horseplay my shorts came down. A few of the other boys caught sight of my penis and from then on I was called "Little Dick". Everyone laughed at the time — even me, although I was inwardly horrified. Looking back on it, that was a crucial mistake — I should have immediately let loose so that the other boys weren't comfortable slagging me — but instead I just laughed along, trying to be good-natured and easy-going.

The next day in school the girls were told about it and from then on people used to call me Little Dick. It was horrendous. I would get posts on my Facebook almost every day about how to enlarge my penis. A girl who I fancied told me she'd be too embarrassed to be with me — I still don't forgive her for that. The whole thing was a nightmare.

I stopped going to school — I just pretended to go and then I would let myself back into our house when my parents went to work. But eventually they found out about that. Consequently I told my parents that I was being bullied but I kept it very vague and when they went into the principal's office I played it all down. I was so embarrassed in front of my Mam and the female principal that I thought the ground would swallow me up.

Finally, one night my little sister told me she had heard what everyone was calling me. She told Mam and the whole thing came out into the open. It was awful but it was also a relief because the adults were all so horrified by the name and all the Instagram shots of little toddlers holding their willies and the penis enlargement ads that sometimes I forgot to be ashamed and I became angry instead.

Eventually, a concerted anti-bullying campaign within the school stopped the bullying. The other kids didn't realise that my mother insisted on a whole series of professionals to come in and speak about bullying. My name was never mentioned in this context but it made the kinder kids more supportive and at least some of the bullies eased off on me. The people who kept on bullying were brought repeatedly to the principal's office — and always with the proviso that they weren't allowed speak or write about me to anyone except their parents. Their parents were also brought in.

I was delighted when things started to improve. I wasn't getting laughed at in class and I didn't get things sent to me on social media so much. Eventually it all just died out.

I don't fit in in that school and I probably never will but I've seen the bullies off and I'm a much stronger person as a result. I have made a couple of friends in the school and I even had a girlfriend for a while. I also have a good connection with my counsellor and I see him every week. I doubt I will ever have to go through such a shaming and horrible experience again; I'm too strong in myself now. I wouldn't let it go on and on.'

Richard, 16

Helping the accidental target

✓ **Address the situation.** The advocate of the accidental target needs to quickly and comprehensively address the bullying environment. There needs to be a continuous and systematic campaign by the parents to ensure that there is a change in the culture so that a small incident doesn't get magnified into a huge life-changing scenario. Parents might need to insist on anti-bullying workshops or that speakers are brought into the school as a matter of urgency.

✓ **Encourage assertiveness.** The parents need to teach the accidental target some ways to assert themselves in the moment or, at least, to honour themselves, and they need to learn it quickly. This might involve the use of force continuum (see Chapter 8) or using assertive eye contact and their strong voice. It won't be easy but it may be necessary.

✓ **Act fast.** Speed is of the essence here as the longer the bullying goes on, the more likely it is that the accidental target's self-esteem plummets and they can no longer even remember what it's like to feel like an ordinary member of the group.

✓ **Gather some inspiration around the target.** Inspiring films such as *The Fat Boy Chronicles*, *Billy Elliot* or *Bully* and books such as *Cat's Eye* by Margaret Atwood or *Bad Girls* by Jacqueline Wilson (see the resources at the end of this book) should be brought into the equation to support the target. Also, the inspiring life stories of famous people (such as the celebrities in Chapter 9) can provide support and inspiration to the target.

✓ **Get outside help.** Counselling and psychotherapy can often bring some much-needed perspective and support to help the accidental target to come through this horrible time stronger than ever before.

Handling difference and promoting tolerance

It's hard to believe that in the twenty-first century we are really so Neanderthal that we cannot treat those with additional needs with the respect and consideration they deserve but, sadly, many children who have 'special needs' are often targeted by other children. Indeed 'special needs' is a term that is often used as an insult among teenagers today, and many children who work with me in the counselling context do their best to make sure that their secret diagnosis of being on the autistic spectrum never gets out. Education, compassion and tolerance are qualities that some families value and that others give little credence to. Yet these are the qualities that need to be cultivated if your child is different from the neurotypicals, especially if they are attending a mainstream school where the social challenges might be that bit tougher. In situations such as these, it is important that the parent ensures that the children in the school are taught tolerance and acceptance and that there are certain programmes in place to ensure difference is respected.

Parents might begin the process of psychoeducation with a series of talks from experts about different conditions. This is a long process but, thankfully, the wind is blowing in this direction anyway so it might be easy enough to convince the school about the need for a programme such as this.

> 'I have autism and I think it was this difference that caused me to be bullied. The bullies used to pretend to be my friends but they weren't at all. They did this because they thought it was funny but I found it frustrating and distressing. I am prone to becoming very interested in certain subjects and when I was in my CSI victims phase, one girl encouraged me to tell everyone how I could get away with murdering each person in the class, individually and in detail. I thought this was an interesting discussion; however, everyone else then decided that I was a potential serial killer. When I look back on my schooldays I can see that this girl was always egging me on to say stuff and do things that were inappropriate. She just wouldn't leave me alone.
>
> In the end my Mum stepped in and insisted that Anti-Bullying Ambassadors were identified in the school. These kids were

supposed to be the upstanders in any bullying incident. While they rarely actually interceded on my behalf, instead they took me under their wing and so I was always occupied with them during lunchtime. They took it in turns to keep a special eye out for me every lunchtime and to give me jobs as part of the gang when I had no one to talk to. I was lucky that my Mum insisted that this initiative was brought in because the girls didn't have much opportunity to gang up on me after that.'

Carl, 23

Victim-blaming and victim-shaming

Victim-blaming is when the victim of a crime is held either entirely or partially responsible for the incident, instead of the perpetrator. The phrase was first coined by William Ryan in his 1971 book *Blaming the Victim* as an ideology that was used to justify racism and prejudiced attitudes towards black people in the United States. But these days, the most typical expression of victim-blaming is the phrase 'asking for it', i.e. the victim of a sexual assault was 'asking for it' because she wore a short skirt and high heels. This sort of 'slut-shaming' has created stormy debates with people as unlikely as Chrissie Hynde of The Pretenders weighing in with her view that girls on a wild night out who are taking drink and drugs shouldn't put themselves in dangerous situations. This, of course, caused controversy as many people quite reasonably pointed out that just because a girl wears short skirts, gets drunk and passes out doesn't give anyone the right to viciously attack and rape her.

Victim-blaming is also often used in the context of a bullying situation. The bully and the sidekicks are often socially sophisticated and they can suavely explain that it was all just larks and high jinks and they blame the victim by explaining to the teacher or the principal that the target just needs to lighten up. Schools are often so horrified and overwhelmed by any accusations of bullying that they are thrilled at the opportunity to get off the hook and so they gladly accept this reasoning. The adults also tend to be shallowly impressed by the highly developed social skills of the bullies and unimpressed by the sometimes more awkward social approach of the target. The school then assures everyone involved it was just horseplay that got out of hand; it was a 'misunderstanding' and it won't happen again. Everyone then walks off, happy that it's all over.

Except for the target. They are often left with a sinking feeling that they didn't honour themselves, that they were somehow to blame and that they shouldn't take themselves so seriously. But it is natural and appropriate to take yourself seriously – our instinct to survive means that we must take ourselves seriously. If we don't honour our feelings and if we allow other people to dismiss us then we can begin to feel that we are unimportant. Feeling like you're unimportant and that your feelings don't matter soon leads the target to feel inadequate and filled with self-loathing.

In a famous series of studies in the 1960s, the social psychologist Dr Stanley Milgram noticed that participants who were ordered to give others electric shocks often criticised the victim in a bid to make themselves feel better about the situation.[21] Follow-up studies back up these findings and it has been found that when people evaluate victims of car accidents, rape, domestic violence, illness and poverty they tend to look for weaknesses in the victims. This is one of the reasons why many people indulge in victim-blaming – we do it in a bid to make negative events controllable and therefore, in our minds, avoidable. We kid ourselves that the victims made a mistake and it was mostly their own fault, really (and so we kid ourselves that it won't happen to us because we won't make such a mistake).

Human beings prefer to believe in a just world where behaviour has consequences that make sense and where we can control what happens to us; a place where nice things happen to nice people and bad things happen to bad people and we reap what we sow.

I wish. The complexity of human nature all too often reminds us that we should be wary of simplifying human interactions. If we can learn to observe other people's suffering as something that could happen to anyone – more 'there but for the grace of God go I' than 'you reap what you sow' – then we can help to make the world a better place by reaching a more complex understanding of any given situation.

Certainly, Roy Baumeister, a social and personality psychologist, argues that it is not always accurate to place all the blame on the perpetrator of a crime.[22] According to Baumeister, 'the myth of pure evil' creates a false idea of ordinary, decent citizens innocently going about their business while crazed, evil and malevolent beasts suddenly decide to round on them and attack viciously. Sometimes the situation is exactly like that but, more often than not, the situation is much more complicated. In any given violent crime, when asked to recall the incident, the perpetrator often tends to minimise the crime while the target tends to maximise it. The truth can generally be found anywhere in between.

This book wouldn't be helpful if it didn't explore how *some* victims – not all, and not even most, but some – have a role to play in their own victimisation. Those who reflexively speak about 'victim-blaming' are missing the point that, in terms of philosophy, this doesn't solve anything. If people blandly say, 'You can't blame the victim. You have to teach bullies not to bully,' without ever pausing to reflect upon the specific dynamic of a given situation, then they are at risk of missing the opportunity to help everyone to relate better.

Self-acceptance and other-acceptance

If you can truly accept yourself and your failings then you can accept other people's fallibility. Some parents can't quite accept their children's personalities; they often cannot handle the fact that their child is in emotional pain and so they deny the very existence of the bullying.

Other parents dream of a different type of child, or they focus on one child and avoid the child who disturbs their heartstrings. Sometimes the child who disturbs their heartstrings is the child who most reminds the parent of their own faults or weaknesses that run in the family — they want a child who is popular and confident and they can't face having a child who is easily intimidated or unpopular. For parents who recognise themselves or their partner in this description, it is recommended that they seriously consider some counselling so that they can come to terms with themselves and their children. Without some level of self-acceptance and other-acceptance, there is little chance of contentment.

The provocative target

The concept of the 'provocative target' can veer dangerously close to victim-blaming and so a certain level of sophistication is required to ascertain the accurate dynamic that is at play in *some* incidents of bullying. The provocative target is characterised by having the tendency to arouse negative feelings such as exasperation, annoyance and irritability in others. This person often lacks the ability to connect effectively with their peers and this is why they are easily singled out. Sometimes, for different reasons, the provocative target is aggressive, has a low tolerance for other people's behaviour and has little empathy or emotional intelligence. Quite simply, they are singled out because they don't have the social skills to understand that their behaviour sometimes drives certain people up the wall and down again.

If the person hasn't got the ability (for one reason or another) to learn social skills, then the school population needs to be taught more tolerance for difference. This can take some time and in the meantime they will need lots of extra support. However, if the child has got some ability to learn, then it can be helpful for the parent to teach their child some social skills that will help them get along more easily with others in their life.

There will always be certain characters who provoke extreme annoyance in others. This can be because the bully feels jealous in the face of the target's abilities, but it can also be because the target tends to boast a little too loudly and a little too often. Some provocative targets can be condescending or filled with feelings of superiority or they might be prone to making poisonous remarks to certain individuals. In circumstances such as this, some people can behave cruelly in the desire to take the provocative person down a peg or two. The teaching of empathy, emotional intelligence and sensitivity to everyone concerned can help to mitigate these circumstances.

'When I think back on why I was bullied in my teen years, I can see why: I was incredibly annoying to many of my classmates. I come from a very academic background and my family taught me to look down upon the uneducated, illiterate fools that made up the bulk of my classmates. Of course this was simply a lesson in how to lose friends and alienate people. I wasn't liked and I made it clear that I didn't give a damn about their opinion of me.

As time went on, however, their understandable dislike slowly turned to bullying as a form of entertainment. At first I could handle it — I gave as good as I got and I often outwitted them with what I believed was a superb display of my verbal talents — but then as the bullies grew in strength and in number, I soon found myself entirely ostracised. I painted myself into a corner with my disdainful and contemptuous attitude and consequently my schooldays became incredibly lonely and painful.

I feel awfully sad when I look back on those days because it was all so unnecessary. I've no idea why my parents thought it was a good idea to cultivate feelings of arrogance and superiority within me; it didn't do me much good at all.'

Philip, 48

Not all of us have the gift of likeability. This doesn't mean that unlikeable people aren't worthy in their own right – Bill Clinton's likeability doesn't mean that he is a 'better' person than Hillary, who doesn't have his gift of charisma. Being popular is mostly important if you are a teenager or if you are running for office; otherwise, it isn't such a great trait. Popular people can sometimes be bland and safe and they may be content to allow the world to keep on turning in whatever way. A highly acclaimed study that followed on from Stanley Milgram's famous work showed us that it is the 'agreeable' people who are more likely to obey orders – even when it means administering electric shocks to a person until they die – while the 'more contrarian, less agreeable personalities' were more likely to refuse to hurt others.[23]

The world needs the opinionated and the argumentative as these people will be the very ones who will stand in the way of terrible acts of evil being committed. However, these strong personalities sometimes need to be harnessed and guided as they are maturing into their personalities.

Some people are so aggressive and competitive that other people just love to hate them. Others are very clever and they know it. They may one day learn to assimilate their intelligence and they may one day be a force for good, but while they are still at school they may not yet have the maturity to handle their powerful intellect.

Inequality, especially unearned inequality, breeds resentment. It also leads to jealousy, and jealousy, in turn, can lead to negativity and even contempt as some rationalise that undeserving people deserve to be hated. Some people are better-looking and they know it. Others still are richer and they know it. When a child is particularly blessed with looks, intelligence, riches or some other enviable aspect of life, the less lucky children can begin to dehumanise them as they wrongly believe that the lucky, superior types don't feel pain or shame in the ordinary way us mere mortals do.

Some provocative targets almost invite bullying by enraging the bullies who become determined to take them down. They might be rude, aggressive, arrogant and condescending and so it is easy for the bullies to spread spiteful remarks about them. (They might also be witty, kind and interesting company, but the potential bullies aren't concerned with this.)

Unfortunately, through a combination of nature and nurture, competitive, clever children who don't have many social skills often have similar parents who are clever and competitive but who are also socially dumb. These kids can often be advised by their parents to retort things like, 'You're just jealous' to the bullies. This rarely ever works, so please don't give your children such misguided advice.

A common problem with the intellectual target is that they often try to fight back by using their intellect – often the very thing that annoyed the bullies in the first place. They can become proud and abrasive. They can also over-think a situation and become paranoid, seeing slights and threats where none were given and be quick to react hurtfully and negatively with a sharp retort. They honestly believe that their towering intelligence will win the day, and if they come up with the 'right retort' they will floor the bullies. But they are often missing the entire point: the targets don't have the social skills to recognise that despite their great academic intelligence, their emotional intelligence is on the floor and they will never win this particular round of child genius.

Studies show that provocative targets are more active, assertive, confident and physically stronger than passive targets. They are often noticeable and sometimes they really bask in the limelight – even when the attention is negative. They can provoke irritation in others and they are also easily provoked themselves. Whereas most targets actively avoid aggressive situations, provocative targets are prone to energetically seek conflict.

> Amelia was an adored only child who was given to boasting about her family's wealth. She often insulted other children in her class who weren't as well-off and who lived in, as she termed it, 'little houses'. Amelia's parents didn't disagree with her opinions about her classmates' homes and often told her that when she was older she would go to private school where she would mix with people of her own social class.
>
> As time went on, Amelia went from being a precocious but funny child to being an unlikeable brat. She was very dismissive of her schoolmates but then she became deeply wounded when they chose not to play with her in the schoolyard. Amelia's mother called the principal requesting that she stop the other children bullying Amelia. The principal was in an awkward position — she could see that Amelia wasn't liked but she also knew that she was creating problems for herself. Most of the kids were scared of Amelia's sharp tongue and kept their distance from her as a self-protective measure. Amelia's parents weren't happy with the weak response from the principal and removed Amelia from the school.
>
> Amelia now attends a private school where, for different reasons — this time it's because the kids are 'cliquey' — she is again having difficulties making friends.

The provocative target is a particularly vulnerable and problematic person and they need more support than others in learning social skills, empathy and consideration. If at all possible, it is important that the provocative target learns more emotional insight. Luckily, this can be taught in a variety of ways. It is important for parents to be aware that there is little use in the blind leading the blind, and if you are lacking in social skills yourself, it might be beneficial to ask someone more adept – such as a counsellor – to help your child. We get extra help for our kids when they have dyslexia or ADHD and so it is also appropriate to get our kids extra help if they need it to help them navigate the social world. It can be useful for parents to view their child's lack of social finesse as a type of 'social dyslexia' – they often don't see what they are missing – but if they are to get on in this world, it is helpful if they can put the work in at an early age to learn these subtleties.

Children who play the victim

There is a saying that bullies teach people to be doormats and doormats teach people to be bullies. Although that seems a bit harsh and simplistic, there is a scintilla of truth in it. If the child has already been bullied in the past and is now facing further bullying, then parents need to be fully cognisant that their child might have developed a pattern of problem behaviour.

Initially, the child might have come to the bullies' notice because of certain tendencies they have, certain expectations of society or certain tendencies the bullies have but, once bullied, some people can then develop the beginnings of a victim mentality that leads to further bullying. Others develop a victim mentality because they learn that playing the victim is the quickest way to gain attention or sympathy. Although this might give individuals some short-term feelings of satisfaction, in the long term, feeling like a victim is an utterly powerless and lonely position to find yourself in.

A little girl I know, Ava, made great friends with another little girl called Caitlin. Caitlin was very popular among her schoolmates but Ava found it harder to make friends. One day Ava told me proudly that she had figured out a way to get Caitlin to play with her every day. 'How so?' I enquired. 'I just stand on the edge of the playground on my own looking very sadly at Caitlin and then I get her,' came the triumphant (although slightly crazed) reply.

At five years of age, Ava had figured out that the easiest way to make friends was to play the victim. This is just one of the many ways that dysfunctional behaviour can develop and become a habit. If Ava's reasoning had continued unchecked she could have gone on to mindlessly play the victim whenever the need arose.

Some children's over-developed sense of importance mixed with their naturally sensitive and emotional disposition can lead them to identify as a victim even when they aren't being victimised. This can be difficult for a parent to penetrate as the parent is trying to provide emotional support to their child and yet the child is becoming increasingly whiny.

So, if a person *feels* bullied and excluded but they actually aren't *being* particularly excluded, how should their parents respond?

Does your child play the victim?

- ✓ **Does the child dislike responsibility?** Refusing responsibility for actions is a classic sign of victim behaviour. A victim has trouble accepting that they might have contributed to a problem and they often refuse to accept any responsibility for the situation. Instead, victims point the finger and ignore their role in having any influence over the problem. If they don't actually think of themselves as victims they often send the message that they are a martyr.

- ✓ **Does your child often feel powerless?** Feeling powerless can be a shadow behaviour, meaning that it isn't obvious and the person doesn't present as powerless but can be manipulative or sly in getting what they need. Habitual victims believe that they are at the mercy of everyone else's decisions. They have an external locus of control (see page 100) and they believe that they are powerless to change their life.

✓ **Does your child have trouble being assertive and setting boundaries?** Victims do not truly believe they can control their life, so they struggle to state what they need, desire or deserve. They have little ability to say 'enough is enough' and their life often consists of repeating patterns of submissiveness, passivity and resentment. If they fail to break this pattern they often suffer from anxiety, depression or other mental health issues.

✓ **Does your child hold on to grudges?** Victims tend to hang on to old grievances. They carry these around as proof that the world is against them and so they believe there is no point in trying to change things. This also gives them a good excuse for not being responsible for their actions. A victim will bring up past history when they were legitimately hurt, and they use these old stories as reasons why they can't make changes to their present circumstances. They may become overly comfortable with their narrative.

✓ **Is your child distrustful of others?** Victims are often suspicious of other people's motives as they suspect everyone else sees the world as they do. This issue is not only a problem of not trusting others; they often don't believe that they are trustworthy themselves and they believe the world is against them.

✓ **Does your child get into arguments easily?** Unless you live in a bigoted or dysfunctional environment or an area of high conflict, there is little reason to have lots of fights with people. Habitual victims have trouble choosing their battles. To them, every battle is a war. They feel under attack all the time and their amygdala is permanently jammed on the fight or flight response.

✓ **Does your child feel excessively sorry for themselves?** Victims have a habit of pitying themselves. Few among us have been untouched by the cruelty of this world, yet some of us cannot seem to move beyond this. They permanently feel like a defenceless child who is unable to fend for themselves. They crave sympathy and they try to evoke sympathy by giving it to themselves. This further traps them in the victim role.

✓ **Is your child prone to blaming others and rationalising?** The serial blamer tends to come up with ever more creative reasons why the world is conspiring against them. Sadly, this tendency to attribute blame to others merely creates a prison for themselves where they feel filled with self-pity and helplessness.

✓ **Does your child tend to focus on the problems?** Do they indulge in long sessions of 'What if?' or 'If only'? Eternal victims occupy themselves with problems and they complain at any given opportunity. They love attention and validation and relish the opportunity to complain.

✓ **Does your child condemn themselves?** If your child is a bit 'woe is me' and prone to saying things like 'I am useless/Everyone is against me/I hate myself' many parents rush to penetrate the wall of negativity erected by the child in a misguided bid to make them feel better in the short term. However, continuously telling your child that they're great when they don't believe it can turn your heartfelt encouragement into background noise. Instead, parents are advised to allow the child to explain why they feel bad, how they feel bad and what is making them feel bad and then offer a rational and thoughtful response to this torrent of emotions. The poet Maya Angelou tells us that 'People will forget what you said, people will forget what you did, but people will never forget how you made them feel.' If you can communicate with your child that they are essentially 'good enough' and 'loved' then this will give the child an inner strength that will ultimately combat feelings of self-loathing and recrimination.

It has been said that over-sensitivity is a preoccupation of the under-occupied. Most people haven't got the time to waste on imagined hurts because they're too busy living their busy lives. As a psychotherapist I have, of course, met clients who are happy to lavish attention on their emotional wounds but aren't willing to spend too much time at all on finding a resolution to their problems. This is a tricky element of my work and, while it is important that the client is given the unconditional positive regard, empathy and congruence that the American psychologist Carl Rogers advocated for, I find it is also helpful for clients to be supported in a quest to find their power.

Locus of control

Studies have shown that people with an 'internal locus of control' rather than an 'external locus of control' tend to be happier and more self-content. An 'internal locus of control' means that the person feels in control of their life events, while with an 'external locus of control' the person believes that their life is under the control of their parents, the school, the government or whoever happens to be in charge at any given moment. People with an internal locus of control are more likely to be motivated to change their life if they aren't happy, while those with an external locus of control are more likely to simply put up and shut up. As a result, their life can become stagnant and they rarely plan to fix their lack of progress in life.

Parents can help their children to develop an internal locus of control by encouraging their children to make decisions for themselves. Some children who feel powerless feel overwhelmed and pressurised by decision-making and so they almost force their parents to make decisions for them. These parents should start in the shallow end by giving their children laughably easy decisions to make — for example, would they like porridge or ice cream? This helps indecisive children who prefer to give their power away to become accustomed to making decisions more easily. As time goes on then parents can help them make more difficult decisions. It is imperative that the parents don't hurry the child through the stages of learning or else the child will feel incompetent and refuse to make decisions.

Not many people make a concerted decision to live an unfulfilled life; not many of us wish to play the victim in a bid to salve our bruised ego. Indeed, most of us begin our lives with high hopes and dreams but then, in this cruel world, it's all too easy to get knocked off track. It is during these golden teachable moments, the moments in life when we either rise to the occasion or fail miserably, that some of us learn from our experiences and others deny or obfuscate so that we don't have to take responsibility. It is a parent's role to teach their children to see challenges as opportunities for life lessons and growth. When a person can take responsibility for their life, when they can source their internal locus of control and when they can accept that they are in charge of themselves, only then are they free to be the master of their fate, the captain of their soul.

If your child tends to play the victim

Teach them how to tap into their power. The parent can help with this by noting the child's strengths and pointing out ways the child can use them. This could be something as random as their ability to listen to others, their ability to notice their deeper emotions or their ability to ask for help when they need it. Parents can then validate their child every time they appropriately use their power.

Encourage them to chase after achievable goals, even tiny goals, so that they can feel the rush of power we all experience when we achieve something. If the parent can help the habitual victim to make a list of small, achievable steps that can work towards a goal in their life then they won't feel so powerless or at the mercy of the big, bad world.

Show them how responsibility can lead to feeling good about themselves. Give reluctant children very small responsibilities such as asking them to buy something for you in the shop. Congratulate them on how well they handled themselves and watch them grow ten feet tall in the process. To build on the success, you can tell them they can keep the change for doing the task so well. Habitual victims need to be held accountable more often so that they become more used to responsibility and so that they don't automatically try to pin the blame on other people.

Guide them towards the funnier side of life and teach them about the concept of playing the victim. Many people who tend to play the victim have forgotten all about their sense of humour; without laughing at your child, as this would be cruel and dismissive, tell them funny (even made-up) stories about other people who tried to play the victim — exaggerated insurance claims or unfair dismissal claims are reported regularly in the newspapers — and how they gave their power away and were left looking foolish. You may need to trawl the net to find these stories, but the 'Stella

Awards' (they poked fun at outrageous and frivolous lawsuits) are a good place to begin.

It is imperative that parents of children who tend to play the victim do not play along with them. They need to refrain from engaging in the blame game, no matter how tempting, or listening eagerly to their stories of woe and misery. These children need to know their parents are there for them and will listen to them but also that their parents are not mindless and will challenge them if necessary and expect them to be accountable for their actions. Although this might seem heartless, in the long run, if parents can support a child to seek satisfaction from within, this will lead them to feel more in control of their life and less likely to succumb to feelings of powerlessness.

Parents need to teach the habitual victim that criticism or a difference of opinion is not such a big deal. The world keeps on turning and the entire conflict might not necessarily even be about them. The victim must recognise that they have a choice whether to allow themselves to enter into petty fights or to take the high road and rise above it.

Perspective is everything. Many people who are given to victimhood tend to 'catastrophise' their situation. This is invariably unhelpful. Sometimes the parent needs to help their child to examine the accuracy of their thoughts. Yes, they've probably not always been ultra-lucky, but neither have they been catastrophically unlucky!

Some kids benefit from creating a 'Good Vibes Jar'. This is where each week the child writes down a good thing that happened to them and puts the note in a jar. When times are bad it can be heart-warming to read through all the nice things that have happened. A gratitude journal can also be effective — the child writes down five things each day that they are thankful for. This sort of project can be used every so often to ensure the child doesn't slide back into playing the victim.

From victim to survivor

When a person feels they are a victim of circumstance, without control over their life, they can soon feel overwhelmed by feelings of powerlessness and self-loathing. Hannah Smith was a 14-year-old girl who took her own life in 2013 after apparently being cyberbullied on the infamous Ask.fm. In the enquiry, it turned out that 98% of the abusive messages were from Hannah herself and only four posts were from actual bullying trolls. Although this may be hard to understand, it is worth noting that 'digital self-harm' is not an entirely new phenomenon, as social media guru danah boyd [sic] wrote in 2010: 'There are teens out there who are self-harassing by "anonymously" writing mean questions to themselves and then publicly answering them.'[24] Teenagers who engage in such self-destructive behaviour need the support of a good psychotherapist as they begin to process such complicated feelings.

Just like going on a mental health diet, small behaviours or small changes in a person's attitude can reap big rewards over time. Eternal victims need to be taught that brooding over grudges holds them down and gives their power away and it is much more helpful to use their power to improve their life. Giving power away is perhaps the most destructive trait of the eternal victim. If you give your power away you allow others to 'make you angry' rather than accepting that other people's behaviour was unreasonable and so you chose to become angry. It might sound like a subtle difference and yet it is incredibly important for a person to understand that no one 'makes' anyone do anything – unless, perhaps, they have a shotgun – instead, we look at the choices offered and we choose the preferred option. We all have the power to be happy today, if we choose to be, yet many of us choose to give our power away and live as if we are forced to live a certain way.

The dance of power between the bully and the target needs to be addressed fully as this destructive relationship can bring out the worst in everyone. Targets of mean kids rarely emerge unscathed from the power play. Some come through the experience bitter and filled with self-doubt and recrimination while others emerge stronger, more self-aware and more able to handle the world than they had been previously. It doesn't make the horrible experience any less; however, once a person has been bullied the only option is to try to get through it with a better sense of self and improved awareness of others. Well-meaning comments advising targets to 'fight back' and 'ignore them' just don't cut it any more. Instead, both parents and children need to commit to an intensive period of reflection and active participation with their place in the world.

In the meantime, the target of bullying needs to balance being kind and compassionate to themselves without tipping into victimhood. To this end, the author Bronnie Ware advises us, 'There is a fine line between compassion and a victim mentality. Compassion though is a healing force and comes from a place of kindness towards yourself. Playing the victim is a toxic waste of time that not only repels other people, but also robs the victim of ever knowing true happiness.'[25]

5

The bystanders
The untapped strength of the upstanders

*'Knowing what's right doesn't mean much
unless you do what's right.'*

Theodore Roosevelt

ystanders need to be hauled from the edges of the drama
and placed slap bang in the centre of it all. Bystanders are the
people who see everything but do nothing. Millions of kids
today are bystanders to cruel bullying, to controlling friendships
and to power plays between stronger and weaker personalities.
They let bullying happen.

The bystanders are the silent majority and yet they hold the
majority of the power. It is estimated that bystanders are present
in 90% of cases of bullying and they can often stop the bullying
within ten seconds if they choose to intervene.[26] The good news
is that if we can obliterate the culture of bystanders, then we will
significantly reduce the impact, the frequency and the duration
of bullying. The bad news is that bystanders, by their very nature,
seldom wish to raise their head above the parapet.

Sophie Scholl was a leading non-violent protestor against the Nazis who was executed in 1943. Scholl's final words still hold truth today: 'The real damage is done by those millions who want to "survive". The honest men who just want to be left in peace. Those who don't want their little lives disturbed by anything bigger than themselves. Those with no sides and no causes. Those who won't take measure of their own strength, for fear of antagonizing their own weaknesses. Those who don't like to make waves – or enemies ... It's the reductionist approach to life: if you keep it small you'll keep it under control.'[27]

Bystanders usually prefer to stay safely in the middle of the road; they are often more easy-going than the personalities who are involved in the drama and they tend to simply hope that everyone will calm down and the nasty behaviour will go away. When interviewed, bystanders often remark that, at the time, they felt plenty of sympathy for the target but they were too scared to act. When called out on it, bystanders often feel survivor's guilt and wish that they had acted more positively to help the situation. The problem is that, all too often, bystanders are let away with their lack of moral courage, and yet, as the author William Burroughs points out, 'There are no innocent bystanders ... what are they doing there in the first place?'

Bullies play to the gallery; they need this gallery and if there is no audience they will turn their attention towards something else. If the bystanders refuse to participate, if they object to the behaviour or find something else to occupy their time, then the fizz goes out of the bullying: bullying without bystanders provides very little of the power they crave.

If we can create an environment where being a bystander means that we are complicit in the drama, then we will eliminate the safe position of the bystanders. Challenging bystanders to become 'upstanders' will change any bullying problem into a more manageable but difficult situation instead of the horrendous epidemic that it is today.

'Looking back, I have to admit that I was a bystander to the bullying that went on when I was growing up. Certain families were targeted by the bullies on my road and their lives were destroyed by the evil hostility shown towards them by the kids on the road. I was generally "in the group", equidistant between the cool kids and the geeks. I said very little when things got mean, but I never actively tried to ease the bullying. I was too scared and too overwhelmed by how nasty it was.

I remember there was this overweight girl, I'll call her "Michelle", and she was a teenager when I was about ten. The kids on the road made her life a misery. Following her up and down the street, making pig noises behind her as she walked. The leaders were always mimicking her voice, pulling at her and laughing at her clothes. She used to look petrified. I remember I used to think "Why doesn't she fight back?" In a way I believed that her lack of fight absolved me of guilt. I didn't have to act to defend her if she didn't try to defend herself. I now realise that she was simply too scared; humiliated, frozen and crushed by our gang of kids. It was really horrible.'

Órla, 34

Even though bystanders don't instigate any attacks, when the bullying is actually taking place, bystanders can be subtle and dismissive in their attitudes and this can cause lasting damage to the target. Bystanders can often be casually cruel by minimising the issue and subtly communicating to the targets that it's not that big a deal or that they had it coming. They do this because they need a coping mechanism to excuse themselves for their inaction.

If we think of the conflict that happens every day in war-torn countries, if we consider the homeless lying on the city streets every day, most of us become overwhelmed, and in classic bystander fashion, we become paralysed by it all. These feelings of helplessness give us an insight into how our children feel when they act as a bystander – it just seems too big and too difficult to face down on our own.

Human nature just can't stomach the more depraved side of our nature – we do it, we watch it, we stand idly by – but we can't really handle it, so we tend to use certain coping mechanisms to pretend that it's not happening. The coping mechanisms of bystanders are complex and varied. Some of us justify bullying behaviour so that we can live with our weak and feeble natures. We may pretend that the target deserved it, that they should stand up for themselves or that others should step in to take responsibility. Bystanders also demonise, dismiss and dehumanise the targets by kidding themselves that the victim doesn't really absorb the bullying the way a normal person would. Bystanders basically kid themselves that it's not really as bad as it looks so they can feel better about not acting.

'The bystander effect'

In the early hours of a cold morning in the Queens neighbourhood of New York on 13 March 1964, a woman called Kitty Genovese drove home from her work as a bar manager to her apartment building. Just before Genovese entered her building, a man named Winston Moseley, a psychopathic serial killer, attacked her and stabbed her twice in the back, then returned later her to attack her again. Genovese later died from her injuries. Two weeks after the event, the *New York Times* published a report describing how up to 38 witnesses saw or heard the attack but did not call the police; people didn't want to get involved in what they wrongly presumed was a drunken quarrel or a lovers' tiff. This incident prompted analyses of the phenomenon that is now known as the 'bystander effect'.

The 'bystander effect' is a social psychological phenomenon that refers to cases in which individuals don't offer help to a victim when other people are present, while if the same individual is in a deserted area they are much more likely to help a victim. It sounds incredible, but the presence of other people reduces the likelihood of a helpful response from a bystander, and not only that, but the greater the number of bystanders, the less likely it is that any one of them will help.

Moral disengagement is used by everyone – bullies, power-hungry friends and bystanders – as a way to reframe behaviour from being unacceptable to being acceptable so that they can give themselves permission to disengage from the morality of a situation.

There are many different ways to morally disengage from a situation: deceiving ourselves about the consequences of our actions, trivialising the situation, embarrassment association, emphasising different priorities and compliance with a norm, pluralistic ignorance, audience modelling, blaming the target, dehumanising the target and the diffusion of responsibility. In all these ways the bystander reframes the behaviour so that the bystanders don't feel complicit and don't feel compelled to act.

Raymond Zack was 53 years old when he decided to wade into the sea to kill himself off Robert Crown Memorial Beach in Alameda, California. His foster mother, Dolores Berry, called the emergency services to say that Zack intended to drown himself. Although the city's firefighters and police responded to the call, they refused to enter the waters. The police thought the firefighters should enter the water to save Zack and the firefighters said that they didn't have appropriate training for this incident (although a later report stated that they did) so they called for a US Coast Guard boat to respond.

In the meantime, as Raymond Zack stood neck deep in water roughly 150 yards offshore, the emergency services squabbled over who was responsible and dozens of civilians on the beach stood watching the drama unfold from the comfort of their beachfront homes. Nobody did anything to help him.

Eventually, after about an hour, Zack collapsed into the water. But even then no one entered the water for several minutes. Finally, someone came to their senses and entered the water and pulled Zack to shore, but it was too late. Zack died in hospital from hypothermia.

If your child is being bullied it can be very helpful if the child can penetrate the bystanders' thinking so that they feel complicit in the drama. If the parents can help the target to figure out in any given situation why each bystander is acting as they are then it will be a good deal easier for the target to penetrate the wall of inaction – the paralysis by analysis – and ask a specific bystander for help in way that will yield positive results. The more we can identify why the bystanders aren't helping, the easier it is to successfully prick the bystanders' consciences and force them to act.

Most people want to be good, but fear often gets in the way. Had Raymond Zack's mother been on the beach and had she methodically gone through the bystanders, looked each person in the eye and calmly but kindly asked them specifically to please wade into the water to help her son, then the response would have been likely to be quite different.

Teaching your children about the bystander effect

Teach your children that their first instinct and the first instinct of those around them will be to deny responsibility for helping the target. Simply being aware of the process can snap a person out of bystander apathy.

If your child is being bullied they can use their knowledge of the bystander effect to penetrate the wall of indifference that seems to surround them. The target of the bullying needs to specifically ask one person to help them — asking the whole room won't get any results, but eyeballing one person and asking them to help you is much more likely to yield results. The child needs to pick one likely-looking individual, look them dead in the eye and tell that one person that they need some help. By picking just one individual the child will then make that person feel responsible and this increases the odds that they will help the child.

It can be helpful for the target to explore and identify beforehand with a counsellor or with their parents who they should pick and ask for help. This person could be pre-identified as the one most likely to offer aid. As a caveat, this potential 'upstander' is unlikely to be from the target's own group of friends — if one of their own friends were upstanders then they would probably have already acted to defend their pal.

Pluralistic ignorance and audience modelling

Pluralistic ignorance describes a situation where the majority of the people in a group privately reject certain behaviour, but assume (incorrectly) that most of the others believe that it's acceptable behaviour. And so if no one responds to nasty behaviour, then bystanders can believe that a response is inappropriate, and so they also refrain from responding.

As we saw with Raymond Zack, bystanders monitor the reactions of other people in an emergency situation to see if others think that it is necessary to intervene. Indeed, when any of us is confronted with the choice to help another person or not we usually attempt first to figure out if they actually need any help. If the situation is ambiguous, we often look to others to see how they are reacting as a way to ascertain the right thing to do. We assume that others know something that we don't, so we gauge our reactions from their reactions. So if those around us calmly allow the situation to continue then we in turn fail to intervene.

Pluralistic ignorance can, of course, take a darker turn when we assume that certain behaviour is appropriate because 'everyone is doing it'. When 40-year-old father of four Matibool was knocked down by a hit and run driver in New Delhi, CCTV footage recorded 403 vehicles driving by over the next 30 minutes – including a police van – without stopping to help Matibool, who lay on the side of the road bleeding to death. Matibool was also ignored by 45 pedestrians – except one who stopped to steal Matibool's phone – until finally a friend came upon the scene and rang for help.[28]

Audience modelling, which is quite similar to pluralistic ignorance, is when people take their social cues from whoever is there in the first place. If there are already some bystanders, then other people will naturally fall into the bystander audience without giving too much thought to their behaviour. In the same way, if there are upstanders acting to support the target, other people will automatically follow suit and protect the target.

For example, if you see a child in the local swimming pool splashing wildly in the water, your first instinct is to look around and see how others are responding. If onlookers appear shocked and are yelling for help you might dive in to help. However, if onlookers are giggling fondly at the child then you will probably follow suit in a bid to avoid looking foolish or hysterical. This seems eminently reasonable on paper and, for the most part, it works very well. However, this tendency to look to others to shape our response can also be quite dangerous and misleading as it leads to the bystander effect.

This often happens in the classroom setting. If a student is confused by the teacher's explanation, their first reaction is to look around the class to gauge if others are confused. If no one else looks puzzled, then, to avoid looking stupid, students will often keep their questions to themselves and everyone assumes that everyone else understands the material. However, if others look confused then the student might quite confidently ask for clarification. (But, sadly, many teens and tweens are incredibly sensitive to looking stupid and often pretend that they understand things that confuse them. So the poor teacher can blithely continue to teach a class where perhaps only one or two students have even a notion of what is going on.)

Situationism is the term used by social psychologists today to describe the way that people's behaviour is determined largely by what's happening around us. Most of us aren't psychopaths or hostile and aggressive maniacs – we are just ordinary people whose behaviour is determined largely by what's happening in our environment.

The problem with pluralistic ignorance, audience modelling and situationism in general is that, according to the highly acclaimed American psychologist Lawrence Kohlberg, only 10–15% of us create our own moral principles; the vast majority of people (85–90%) fall in with the moral norms of society.[29] So in a bullying or power play situation, if others are laughing along at the cruel jokes then the bystanders assume that this is acceptable. Sadly, often a combination of pluralistic ignorance and audience modelling is usually at play and the most common thought processes are often incorrect, and everyone's behaviour is misleading.

In a famous study of the bystander effect, social psychologists Bibb Latané and John Darley asked participants in their study to complete a questionnaire. After a few minutes, smoke started to emerge from underneath a door in the back of the room. Some participants were alone in the room when this happened, but for other participants in the study, there were two other decoy students pretending to be completing questionnaires in the room as well. The decoy students were instructed to keep calm no matter what happened. The results showed that when the participants were left alone, 75% of them left to report the smoke, but when the decoys were in the room continuing to calmly fill out the questionnaire, only 10% left to get help. In some cases, the smoke got so thick the participants could barely even read the questionnaire, yet as long as the bystanders remained calm, the participants followed suit and presumed that they should also remain calm – and ignore the smoke.[30]

How to combat pluralistic ignorance and audience modelling

If your child is guilty of being a bystander but is too scared to take on the bullies, it is helpful if they can simply speak to the target in a normal way whenever possible. This might be whenever the bullies aren't around or, better, it might be when they are. The point is that your child learns that the target needs help, that the situation isn't funny and that their mental reframing of the situation is inaccurate. It doesn't have to be a dramatic about-turn, just a sympathetic word given regularly and openly to the target so that your child penetrates the wall of pluralistic ignorance and audience modelling that is shaping the bystanders' behaviour. Likewise, if the attacks are happening online, your upstanding child can choose to add a kinder comment instead of more poison.

The diffusion of responsibility

The diffusion of responsibility has a similar result to pluralistic ignorance – lots of people acting as bystanders – but for different reasons. The diffusion of responsibility is when actions committed by a member of a group are considered the responsibility of 'the others' instead of the individual. The problem with the diffusion of responsibility is that the more witnesses (or bystanders) present, the less responsible each individual feels. If you are the only eyewitness present, 100% of the responsibility rests on your shoulders, but if there are ten other eyewitnesses present the responsibility becomes diffused among the group members and so only 10% of the responsibility is yours.

When six girls bully one boy, the ringleader might defend herself by saying, 'Why am I the only one who is being punished? The others were doing it too!' To the ringleader this is a rational defence. She isn't responsible – she believes that she is technically only one-sixth responsible (even when she knows intuitively that she led the group and the other five were following her lead).

It was the home-coming dance in Richmond High School, California in 2009 and a 16-year-old girl, wearing her brand new sparkly lavender dress, told her father that she would see him when he picked her up after the dance. When the father got a vulgar phone call at 10.52 p.m. from a man saying his daughter was great at sex he immediately went into panic mode. Even so, he hoped it was just a silly high school prank and had no idea of the horror that lay before him.

An hour later the father saw his daughter, lying on a hospital trolley, barely conscious and at death's door, after being gang-raped for up to two and a half hours by a group of up to 20 males.

The males had been drinking in a dark courtyard on campus and when the teenage girl went outside to get some air she was propositioned for sex. When she refused, she was continuously beaten and raped for 2½ hours. At least 24 bystanders watched the assault, while many of them allegedly laughed, cheered and took photos of the assault on their mobiles instead of calling the police.

The following is a description of the assault by a bystander: 'They were kicking her in her head and they were beating her up, robbing her and ripping her clothes off; it's something you can't get out your mind. I saw people, like, dehumanizing her; I saw some pretty crazy stuff. She was pretty quiet; I thought she was like dead for a minute but then I saw her moving around. I feel like I could have done something but I don't feel like I have any responsibility for anything that happened.'[31]

Eventually, an 18-year-old girl heard of the attack from her boyfriend and immediately contacted the police. The victim was found unconscious and was taken to hospital in a critical condition.

Twenty witnesses to the event appeared before the court and six out of seven of the defendants were eventually charged. In January 2011 the victim, who weighed only 100 pounds at the time and had apparently never drunk alcohol before the incident, received a monetary settlement of $4 million from the school district.

Many of us are guilty of diffusing responsibility. If we think that someone else can step in to stop a troubling situation, then we tend to believe that we can take a step back from it. And so we may wring our hands about the trouble in various war-torn countries and say 'something should be done', but when nothing is done we assume the fault lies with the millions of others who also believe that 'something should be done'.

The presence of other people actually inhibits our decision to speak out or help. There are many social experiments on YouTube that parents can safely show their children which film people calmly stepping over corpse-like bodies on the floor. If parents show these clips to their kids then the children will better understand and combat the bystander effect.

Latané and Darley also explored the phenomenon of the diffusion of responsibility in a social psychology experiment. In this study the participants were invited to take part in a group discussion over an intercom system. For some of the participants it was a one-on-one conversation and for others it was a conversation with a group of five other people. During the discussion, one of the voices on the intercom said that he was having a seizure and called for help (this was a pre-recorded set-up). Of the people who believed they were the only one who heard the voice, 85% called for help, but when the participants believed they were one of six people who heard the voice, only 31% of the participants called for help. Follow-up interviews suggested that the bystanders who didn't act *did* feel concerned but didn't feel responsible enough to do anything about it. (Interestingly, when they were asked, most of the bystanders disagreed that the presence of others had influenced them.)[32]

How to help when diffusion of responsibility occurs

The tiny glimmer of hope here is that if someone is courageous enough to step up to the plate and help, then the situation will relatively quickly be swarmed with would-be helpers. We just need one courageous person to morally engage in situations where the bystander effect occurs and it can break the chain.

Once the chain is broken others will follow suit, often gladly and helpfully. One action from one courageous person can set the groupthink in a different direction, it can prick people's conscience and, once the herd has decided to be helpful, the herd will go to

> extraordinary lengths to show themselves and others how kind they can be.
>
> If the school can promote anti-bullying ambassadors and that it 'just takes one', and if the culture of being an upstander is both recognised and rewarded, then the bystanders begin to be perceived as being part of the problem and lazy bystanders can no longer presume that they are innocent of any wrongdoing.

Children are trained these days to look to the nearest adult for direction and so they have little experience in standing up and taking a moral stance in a situation. The problem with this is that, among children, the really nasty bullying generally takes place well out of the sight of any supervising adult or is conducted by the supervising adult. Not only that, but adults are accustomed to refraining from intervening in any situation involving children who are not theirs. When British police left a five-year-old girl alone in a busy shopping centre and told her to 'look lost', 600 people walked by before an adult approached to help her.[33] If a child is crying we aren't inclined to try to help the child these days – instead we tend to look for the parents – despite being told that 'it takes a village to raise a child', adults these days, for various reasons, are often afraid to take responsibility over other children. Sadly, the culture of standing idly by is alive and well in the modern era.

When Tara, 14, was being mocked by some boys before class for having 'turkey legs', she looked one of her friends, who was a bystander, straight in the eye and asked her if she thought her legs looked weird. The friend said no, she didn't. But she then ruined it all by muttering, 'God, I don't know why you're asking me!' Tara then asked another person, who wasn't a friend but had been pre-identified in her sessions with her counsellor as a strong personality who had a high level of moral engagement, what she thought about the boys' comments.

The pre-identified, morally engaged person said nothing there and then, but she took on the challenge and as soon as the class began, she told the teacher that the boys were picking on Tara. Tara was pleased with this result as she didn't look like a rat and the upstander was robust and popular enough to be able to fend off any attacks from the bullies at the back of the class. Tara's quick reaction successfully stopped the taunting and sent potential bullies the clear message that she wasn't someone who would be easily bullied.

Deindividuation

Deindividuation is when people who are part of a group lose touch with their identity, their view of themselves and their sense of morality and begin to align themselves more closely with the group's ethical standard. 'Ten bodies, one head' is the phrase that best describes deindividuation. Indeed, the old Monty Python joke comes to mind – in the film *Life of Brian*, Brian declares to the mob, 'You're all different,' and one voice pipes up, 'I'm not.'

The problem here is that, apart from social, charitable or religious organisation, like the Scouts, most groups don't actually have an ethical standard. Usually what brings a group together is some ideal image such as winning the cup (or, indeed, getting an education). In cases like this, many of the mob look to the strongest personalities in an attempt to emulate the personality of the group.

If your child has a high need to fit in they are liable to copy other kids' behaviour, and they may sweep aside their morals in a bid to feel part of it all. Sometimes, depending on the context, the group ethics can default to a minimum standard of behaviour, setting a new low for acceptable behaviour. If a group of teenage boys enjoy playing violent video games together, their views of what is socially acceptable can be lowered as a consequence of the video games and their subsequent mob mentality. The video games give them an identity of being tough and cruel and they now behave like this so as to fit in with this ideal. The individual morality deteriorates and the kids align themselves with what they consider to the group's identity. They can then become desensitised to bad behaviour, especially when they are teenagers and the need to fit in is at the forefront of their brain.

This is a dangerous but very common scenario that parents need to watch out for. It is not that being in with a group of boys who enjoy playing violent video games is an inherently 'bad' thing to do; it is that if a group of boys whose identity is centred on these video games exist within a bullying environment then a lot of nasty behaviour can be perceived as acceptable.

Blaming the target and blaming others

Blaming everyone else is another aspect of the private and twisted logic that allows bystanders to live with themselves as they watch someone's life being destroyed. If the person who is being bullied isn't a good friend of the bystander, then the bystander (in a bid to convince themselves that their own inaction is reasonable) can always think of other people who should step in before them. Many bystanders have different priorities and they are simply too wrapped up in their own lives to have the empathy or the moral engagement to care sufficiently to put their head above the parapet and come to the rescue in any given situation. Bystanders are generally keen to pass the buck on to someone else – someone who is a better friend of the target, someone who holds greater responsibility or is more popular or whatever you're having yourself.

In the course of my work, I often meet with teenagers who have been bystanders in a bullying situation. The fizzing indignation and moral outrage that revs up these kids would be comical if it wasn't so sad. For a moment these teenagers feel like latter-day Martin Luther Kings in their fight against evil as they pinpoint who exactly is to blame and who should make more tangible efforts to defend the target. They rationalise the situation by repeating to themselves that the target isn't very close to them so it's a case of 'not my circus, not my monkeys' – but if it was, oh they would be magnificent!

Sometimes the bystanders don't like the bully's behaviour but they prefer the bully to the target – indeed, they might be friends with the bully, as it is not at all unusual for a young person to witness a good friend bullying another weaker individual who is also part of their group. In these situations, bystanders often make the popular but morally weak decision to stick with the powerful friend instead of pointing out that certain behaviour is not acceptable.

How to help when blame is getting in the way of positive action

The degree of responsibility a bystander feels is usually shaped by the relationship between the bystander and the victim. However, people also decide to become upstanders based upon whether they feel the target is deserving of help and whether they feel competent enough to help. If parents can teach their children that every child deserves help, that bullying is always wrong and, most of all, that there is always something a person can do to help, then the boundaries are clear.

This can be taught in a myriad of different ways — walking down a city street can begin thoughtful conversations about the homeless, and TV programmes and books can provoke conversations about how people aren't always nice but that doesn't give us permission to allow them to be treated badly. The conversation can then move on to helping those less fortunate than ourselves.

When people point the finger of blame it is often because they haven't learned to accept responsibility for themselves. Responsibility should be taught slowly but surely as the child develops. With our current 'generation snowflake', many parents are reluctant to give their children much responsibility, and yet, when kids are taught responsibility in a positive manner, the new freedom and control over their life choices often makes the child feel much better about themselves.

Taking responsibility for our actions can be very empowering. Being accountable enables us to leave behind the effort that denial or blaming takes and to instead focus that energy on new behaviour that will produce a more effective and successful outcome in the future. When a person accepts responsibility, suddenly the power to improve and succeed lies with them.

Equally, when a person blames others, they are giving their power away, allowing themselves to believe that 'other people' have the power to improve their world.

Encourage your child to take some responsibility for any situation — when you're at the shops, leave it up to one child to be in charge of getting the bread and another child has to get the loo roll. It doesn't matter how big or small the responsibility is, what matters is that they get used to the feeling of the burden being placed upon their shoulders.

The key to teaching your child to take responsibility isn't to jump in and save them if they are about to make a mistake, nor is it to harangue them if they fail. Teaching responsibility in a positive manner involves cheering them on when they succeed and teaching them that failure in a task doesn't really matter — the world keeps turning and the sun can still shine even if we forget the bread.

Many of us do this habitually as adults also, but as adults we aren't confronted with the same level of barbaric cruelty that teenagers are faced with – for example, grown-ups don't tend to slut-shame or spread nasty rumours on social media as often or as rabidly as immature teenagers do. Not only that, but teenagers often haven't the skill set to be able to handle a situation where their friends are behaving badly – they can't quite face the fact that they shouldn't sit idly by as their friend behaves cruelly but they aren't willing to admit that their friend is in the wrong either – and so they reframe the situation to give it a more palatable interpretation; they tell themselves the target deserved the treatment.

This is a difficult situation for even an adult to handle but it arises much more often in the teenage years, when they haven't yet learned to filter out the people that they view as morally reprehensible and remain friends with the people who share their own moral viewpoint. In addition, as adults not so many of us are forced to work beside the same 100 or so individuals for five years, five days a week. It is a very intense environment and it behoves many teenagers to be quite political about their friendships if they are to survive school. Sustaining relationships in the face of conflict is no mean feat and yet it is something that needs to be taught to our children as it is a key element to building character.

'Looking back I was complicit in the bullying that took place in my school when I was younger. There was a girl who was universally disliked. She was very good-looking and she was very good at school. She was also arrogant and made sure that everyone knew just how successful she was at everything. She had a well-developed bitchy streak and I, just like everyone else, had fallen victim to some of her malicious comments. When she got a bit older, in third year I think, she got a reputation with the boys as she apparently got drunk one night and was with two different boys at the same time.

I think we were all delighted when the boys began calling her a slut. She was just too perfect, too good-looking and I think we all got a guilty thrill out of seeing her taken down a peg or two. But as time went by the photos and the snaps on social media became very spiteful. But it was all funny and so I couldn't help "liking" the comments.

It kind of took on a life of its own. There were a few dodgy shots of her with her top off doing the rounds; she was comatose in the shots and she looked rotten in them so it was really awful. I suppose I was as guilty as anyone else but what can you do? You

> get sent ugly pics of an annoyingly beautiful girl and you make a funny comment. At the time I just thought she was a complete fool to get herself into such a bad situation.
>
> It's only years later when I piece together what actually happened that I remember that there were lots of rumours that she used to self-harm. She eventually died by suicide when we were in sixth year. She took loads of pills one night when her parents were away. Horrible story really, everyone felt really guilty.'
>
> Joanne, 20

Bystander fear and lack of confidence

Some bystanders are afraid – with good reason – that if they say anything they will be turned on by the bullies. For young people, it is a very real possibility that doing the right thing for someone else will equate to doing the wrong thing for their own social status. As one teenage girl I worked with memorably pointed out, 'I can't be nice to Allie because she is a loner and if I'm friendly with her then I'll be classed as a loner too.'

Barbara Coloroso explains in her book *The Bully, the Bullied, and the Bystander* that it's a dog-eat-dog world among teenagers who are viscerally aware of their social status.[34] If standing up to bullies means risking their own popularity, most teenagers will keep schtum. It's simply not worth it and the teenager comforts themselves by thinking (logically enough) it's not their responsibility and that it's the adults who should put a stop to it. The teachers are expected to be able to magically stop the bullying, yet the primary focus of teacher training is learning to teach and so the teacher justifies their inaction by thinking (also logically enough) that bullying – especially cyberbullying – is outside their remit. Of course, many schools are at a loss as to how to handle the countless episodes of bullying that occur every term and these feelings of overwhelmed helplessness can often lead to a defensive dismissal of accusations of bullying. Sadly it is the target who is then left to carry the can as a consequence of the spinelessness of everyone else – and, all too often, the target doesn't have the self-protective qualities that enable them to withstand the bullying behaviour.

How to help when fear inhibits the bystanders

Bystanders are easily intimidated — they don't realise that they have a power of their own and if all the bystanders grouped together they would usually far outweigh the strength of the bullies. Parents need to teach their children the difference between appropriate fear — when a crazed axe murderer is looming over them — and inappropriate fear — when a person feels needlessly frozen by another person's words.

If your child is too fearful to openly confront the bullies, they can instead take on the role of the 'distracter'. This is when the bystander, realising that a mean moment is about to unfold, distracts people away from it. This can be very effective.

When children feel competent and capable in the world then they will have the confidence that what they do can make a difference in the world. This doesn't mean that they have to face down the bullies directly — there are many ways to skin a cat and an empowered and savvy child will find a way to be self-protective but still make a difference. (If your child has a tendency to take on the bullies in an unsafe manner then this is an issue that needs to be addressed. Being foolhardy in the face of aggression is neither helpful nor self-protective and this child probably needs to be guided towards a safer path. If this brave child can be helped to safely assert themselves then parents have seriously helped their child.) The gift of feeling confident and competent is a lasting legacy that parents can bestow upon their children that will not only give them the confidence to make an impact on bullying but will also empower them to steer their own ship during the course of their life.

Dehumanising the target

In March 1993, the award-winning photographer Kevin Carter took a harrowing photo of an emaciated Sudanese girl being watched by a vulture who was waiting for the starving girl to die so that he could eat her. Carter later reported that he waited 20 minutes for the vulture to spread his wings and during this time the starving child whimpered and panted but Carter did nothing to help her. When asked about the incident he said that he took the picture because 'it was his job title'. He had been told not to touch the child because of fear of transmitting disease.

In the end he took the photo, scared the vulture away, gathered his belongings and went about his business. He didn't help the crawling child and had no idea if the child lived or died. Carter later explained that he 'didn't want to get involved'. (The very next year Carter won the Pulitzer Prize for the photo but he later became overwhelmed by a combination of money problems and haunting, vivid memories of 'killings and corpses and anger and pain' and he killed himself in his truck in Johannesburg by carbon monoxide poisoning.)

Many of the Jewish people in Nazi Germany were similarly dehumanised by ordinary German citizens. The residents of the towns beside the concentration camps knew what was happening but they reframed the situation so that they didn't view the Jews as real people. Ireland too has a history of bystanders and dehumanisation. The ordinary people were well aware of what was happening in the industrial schools and the so-called Magdalene laundries. They knew the treatment of these children and women was inhumane, but rather than acting against it, the people tended to write them off as little animals who needed little more than a lock and chain.

How to help when dehumanisation occurs

Shakespeare evidently understood the process of dehumanisation as we see in *The Merchant of Venice* when Shylock speaks to Salarino about the Jewish people and asks plaintively, 'If you prick us, do we not bleed? If you tickle us, do we not laugh?'

The most effective method to break the tendency to dehumanise people is to simply start treating the target like a human being. Refuse to pretend that they aren't 'like us'. Look at your peers blankly when they assume that you too view this person as 'different'. Speaking to the target works very effectively as a simple conversation reminds everyone involved that the target is an ordinary person. The dynamic changes immediately when one person chooses to go to the target and speak to them. It can be about the weather, their holidays, school stuff; it really doesn't matter so long as it isn't incendiary to the bully — keep the conversation to benign subjects and start chatting. Immediately the bully's steam will be reduced and the bystanders will be reminded that the target is an ordinary person, just like themselves.

When parents and teachers are the bystanders

Neutrality in times of injustice is immoral. Archbishop Desmond Tutu cleverly pointed out, 'If you are neutral in situations of injustice, you have chosen the side of the oppressor. If an elephant has its foot on the tail of a mouse, and you say that you are neutral, the mouse will not appreciate your neutrality.'

Parents and teachers can also be the bystanders by being 'neutral' when neutrality is an inappropriate and cynical response. Parents and teachers can collude by dismissing or underplaying the situation. This 'don't be so sensitive' attitude is not only heartless, it can be more destructive than that because parents and teachers are supposed to have moral authority. When a target of bullying is told that they are in the wrong and it is their neurotic personality that is at fault – not the bullies' obstreperous aggression – it leads the target, who may already feel insecure and threatened, to feel that they are to blame. The far-reaching consequences of this can be soul-destroying.

If a certain interaction is tacitly – or even openly – approved by the school authorities, then it will take a very strong and confident personality to be able to stand up to that culture. Many teenagers who I work with in the counselling context complain that the teachers and the principal allow the bullying and controlling to continue. However, if the teachers look the other way while there is a bullying dynamic, then it is even worse than the bystander effect as the teachers have a good deal of authority and they are setting the tone. If the parents see this happening, although they should call the school out on it, they should probably refocus their efforts on supporting their child in other ways without expecting massive help from the school administration. The fact is that if the school authorities tacitly allow bullying to take place they are unlikely to suddenly rise up and declare a war on bullying. Nevertheless, a continuous stream of formal complaints will certainly keep the situation in check while you assess the position. (See more about whether to change schools in Chapter 8.)

> *'I'm gay and I'm one of those people who always knew it. The amount of gay people who I know who were bullied in school just for being gay is incredible. When I was really young I was just called a "sissy". But as I got older it turned darker and more homophobic. When I was in third year I had a pig of a teacher who seemed to resent my very existence. He was a clever bully. He led the attacks in a clever way. He would ask leading questions and then smirk wickedly when the other kids would inevitably follow his lead and call me "faggot" or "queer". I was deeply disturbed by his behaviour.*
>
> *It's hard to put into words, but I felt if the people in charge thought it was OK to bully and insult me for being who I was then that meant I was fundamentally unacceptable. Unfortunately, that feeling of being "wrong" has never quite gone away. Not only that, but I felt very unsafe in his class. I knew that he didn't like me and I knew that he encouraged the other boys to hate me. It was very threatening and it was the most distressing year of my life.'*
>
> *Stephen, 35*

Sometimes it is even worse than this and the teacher is a blatant bully. This happens more often than parents think and at times like this it is essential that parents step up to the plate and get ready to make a robust complaint to the school administration. If you complain, by email and with a request for a meeting, each and every time there is an incident with the teacher, you will eventually get a response. Although it is very unlikely that your child will be moved from the bullying teacher's class, if you are a powerful advocate, the bullying teacher will be strongly advised to lay off your child.

Empowering your child to be an upstander

We need to teach our children to take responsibility, and that if no one else is doing it then it is our job to intervene. The barriers to intervening might seem limp and childish to adults — and maybe they are — but they are very real barriers for children and this is why the bystanders are allowing the bullying to flourish.

Kids need specific instructions on how to report bullying or nasty behaviour in a clever and effective manner so that it won't all blow up in their faces. Parents also need to explain to their children that if they are a bystander then they are complicit in the action that is taking place. Teachers can play a role by exploring the bystander effect in Nazi Germany, and parents can download relevant social experiments from YouTube for their kids.

Parents can build an upstanding sensibility in their children by asking thoughtful questions about their children's lives. From a very young age parents can ask if they saw anyone who needed help today and if there was anything your child could have done about it. This might entail your child playing with a kid who was left alone or being kind to one who was mocked by bullies. The point of the exercise is that the parent teaches the child that they can have an input into any situation and this can either be a positive or a negative input.

The good news is that teaching your child to be an 'upstander' gives them improved emotional intelligence, a sense of confidence and an internal locus of control, which has a direct influence on their ability to be happy. It also teaches a sense of responsibility to the child which will stand them in good stead in their future.

Gentle and continuous communication is key here as you ask your child, 'Was any child left out of the games today? Did you try to include anyone who looked lonely?' This teaches the child that it is within their remit to help any child who looks lonely or sad. Of course it won't always work, but with some communication with their parents, the child can feel satisfied that they did their best.

The bystanders in Nazi Germany

The Holocaust could arguably be considered the most important moral lesson that we can learn about the devastating impact of the bystander. 'We were just following orders' has now gone into the lexicon as a prime example of the typically mealy-mouthed excuse of the bystander.

During the early 1930s, Germany was experiencing great economic and social hardship. Inflation, unemployment and economic instability were rampant and the country was on its knees. This created an atmosphere of insecurity, competitiveness and unhappiness: the perfect bullying environment (see Chapter 6).

The weaker members of society were anxious to create stronger bonds with the stronger members of the community, trust was scarce and the survival instinct was highly aroused. At this fragile time, the weaker people would have been open to any suggestions uttered by stronger personalities to make the pack – Germany – stronger. Unfortunately for the world, the most charismatic leader – and bully – of this period was a man called Adolf Hitler.

It wasn't for random reasons that Hitler used the Jewish community as a scapegoat; many people blamed the Jews for Germany's economic and social problems and so, when Hitler promised, in his powerful and influential manner, that the Nazi Party would resolve these issues, many Germans sat up and listened. The simplicity of the answer to Germany's economic hardship – blame the Jews – was alluring to people who weren't interested in analysing and exploring the long-winded and vague discussions that more accurately – albeit less dramatically – examined the economic crisis.

The persecution of the Jews began systematically. At this point many members of the public were content that the Nazi policies were improving their economic system – not only that, but some people prospered when the Jews were dispossessed of their property. As time went on and the policies became more punitive, many Germans were mostly relieved that the brutal attacks weren't impacting their own families and continued to act as bystanders; they were afraid to speak out because of the sheer brutality of the Nazi regime.

The pack instinct to preserve and protect the purity of the group was utilised to a significant degree with eugenics as the Nazis argued that Jews, Roma, Sinti (Gypsies), black people and people with disabilities were a serious biological threat to the German-Aryan people. These tin pot theories convinced the bystanders that Germany would prosper as one homogenous group of 'pure-blooded' German-Aryan people.

The vast majority of the people who lived in Germany became aware of how the Nazi regime was treating the Jews. However, not many took an active position to help; classic bystanders, they may not have openly persecuted the Jews but they didn't actively help them either.

So while it could be argued that the bystanders inside Germany allowed the persecution of the Jews to continue, the citizens of the world also acted as bystanders; they didn't lobby their governments to act when it was morally correct to do so and the political leaders of the world were also bystanders as they didn't act to prevent Hitler from continuing with his evil regime. As a direct consequence of the inaction of bystanders, Europe was unprepared for the terrible might of the Nazi regime when Hitler invaded Poland.

The residents of the villages near the camps at Dachau, Buchenwald, Bergen-Belsen, Sachsenhausen, Mauthausen and Ravensbrück, to name but a few, were perfectly aware of the atrocities and horror that happened inside the camps. The stench coming from them was intense, and Allied soldiers reported smelling camps from as far as 20 miles in a certain wind. The Allies later accused the German citizens of these towns of knowing full well what was happening and yet making no effort to save one life. Consequently, as punishment for their passivity, after the war they were forced to clean up the emaciated corpses and bury them in mass graves.

Most individuals in occupied Europe did not collectively help the victims of Nazi policies. Except for the Danes.

In the context of the political climate at the time, the strong stand taken by Denmark was courageous.

Denmark was the only occupied country that actively resisted the Nazi regime's attempts to deport its Jewish citizens and their response is considered proportionately the largest action of collective resistance to the aggression of Nazi Germany. In all, 7,220 of the 7,800 Danish Jews and 686 of their non-Jewish relatives were smuggled safely out of Denmark as a direct consequence of the moral courage of their defenders. The Danish resistance movement was all the more unique because it was nationwide; in striking contrast, the French Resistance was an underground movement littered with betrayal and suspicion.

The Danish Jews were provided with underground escape routes, false papers, food, clothing, money and sometimes even weapons by their fellow countrymen. Their resistance wasn't completely successful as approximately 464 Danish Jews were deported to the Theresienstadt ghetto in Czechoslovakia. Yet, even so, all but 51 Danish Jews survived deportation, largely because Danish officials put pressure on the Germans concerning the well-being of the Danish Jews who had been deported. More than 99% of Danish Jews survived the Holocaust. When we look at the horror that happened all over Europe at the time, the Danes proved that, with the right mindset, the collective might of 'upstanders' can be very powerful.

Of course many other brave heroes in other countries also tried to save Jewish people. Yet it is the unity of the Danish people during the Nazi regime that reminds us that the 'upstander' mentality can make a real difference. Unlike other countries, the Jewish Danes were well integrated into the community and so the Danes perceived the attack by the Nazis as an affront to all Danes. The Danes were brought up to value close-knit communities and so their response was in keeping with their values. A less cohesive group would be unlikely to have responded in a similar fashion. The cohesiveness, confidence and moral engagement of the Danes shows us how the values that are important in a group can have a critical impact on the behaviour of the group.

'Be the arrow, not the target'

President Higgins quoted the words of the Welsh academic Raymond Williams when he advised the youth of Ireland to 'be the arrow, not the target' and this is exactly the type of upstanding mentality that needs to be fostered among children today.[35] Compassion, empathy and other valuable traits can be taught by parents so that bystanders feel connected to bullied children in a compelling way – even when they don't much like the bullied children. Children need to learn that no one should be mistreated and that whoever is present in the face of mistreatment needs to act or stand accused of being guilty.

Lack of connectivity is a growing issue. So many of us are living in virtual reality that we have little ability to connect with our peers 'in real life', which leads to a lack of empathy and understanding in society. Lack of empathy and connectivity was offered as a possible explanation of the sad death of two-year-old Wang Yue in China. 'Little YueYue' had wandered out of her parents' apartment while her mother was doing the laundry and she was tragically knocked down by a van. The toddler lay dying on the ground for several minutes as 18 people walked by her without stopping. Then another car drove over her and eventually a woman (a scavenger) came across Little YueYue and tried to help. It was reported that the apathy was a consequence of the lack of community or connectivity in the migrant neighbourhood and a 'Stop Apathy' campaign was immediately launched as a response.

Telling your child stories about bystander apathy will help them to understand the role we all play in the fight between good and evil, and teaching empathy is an easy and effective way to instil humanity and kindness in your children. This will help with their emotional intelligence which in turn is proven to help in many aspects of people's lives. If parents can teach children that we all have the choice to be part of the problem or part of the solution, then your children will, in turn, acquire the emotional depth to realise that everything we do has consequences. The anti-Nazi dissident and theologian Dietrich Bonhoeffer nailed it when he explained the far-reaching impact of bystanders: 'Silence in the face of evil is itself evil ... Not to speak is to speak. Not to act is to act.'

6

The bullying environment
Group cohesion and competitiveness

*"The only thing necessary for the triumph of evil
is that good men should do nothing."*

Edmund Burke

Many of us have experienced the feeling of being in a potentially bullying environment; a milieu where everyone present feels insecure of their position, where there is a heightened feeling of competitiveness, a strict hierarchy and a dogmatic approach to life. Within this sort of atmosphere people can become irritable and scrappy from the relentless strain of competition and many start to look for mindless forms of entertainment. For a dominant personality within a competitive environment, demonstrating their power over others is the most natural option; and so, very often, bullying begins to occur.

In socially difficult environments, communication quickly becomes a nervous affair as everyone fears saying the 'wrong' thing. This is because, with so many insecure individuals fighting for a place in the pecking order, molehills can all too easily be turned into mountains as the slightest remark can seem like a cruel dig.

Small, nasty power plays occur and insecurity becomes even more rampant as everybody then feels even more precarious in their position.

If the environment encourages everyone to compete with one another, then our amygdala can feel almost permanently activated and so everyone responds depending on their tendency to fight, flight, freeze or appease. The stage is set quickly and from then on it's a dog-eat-dog world where each person becomes either part of the problem or part of the solution: some become the alpha personalities, some become the crew, the targets are mercilessly picked out for random reasons and the bystanders begin to align themselves in the power play.

If you are the parent of a child who is being bullied or in a difficult relationship dynamic then it is important that you examine the environment where it all started. Whether in school or online, the more you can begin to comprehend the environment, the easier it will be for you to help your child to either adapt to the environment, change the environment or leave the environment. Not only that, but the parent also needs to understand the dynamics that are at play. Is one person in the drama hungry for power? And can their need for power be directed in a more positive fashion? Is another person in the drama enjoying their important position as sidekick? Are the bystanders enjoying their horror at the drama of it all? These are difficult questions to answer at a glance but as you examine all the intricacies of bullying, exclusion and difficult relationships, it soon becomes clear that the more you can understand the situation, the easier it is to manage it.

One of the lessons we can learn from Stephen King's harrowing account of Dodie is that if a person is operating within a bullying environment then they need to become conscious of the social norms around them. Parents of gentle children need to ensure that they don't mindlessly place their kids in competitive atmospheres with the vague hope that they 'grow a pair'. This is not playing to the child's strengths and it will merely create an insecure and emotionally volatile individual.

Although the common narrative is that we should tell our kids to 'be yourself' and 'don't mind about the bullies and they won't mind about you', for potential targets who are attending a competitive school that tends to turn a blind eye to bullying this is dangerous advice. Instead, sadly, it is socially appropriate for kids in certain environments to be on the lookout for the social mores of the group so that they can adapt and so that don't inadvertently rattle any cages.

There is little point in asking your child to be a martyr for society's ills. If you want to give your child the freedom to be themselves then make sure not to put them in a bullying environment. If circumstances dictate that you have to send them to a specific school where bullying often takes place then the least a parent can do is equip them for this difficult environment. This doesn't mean that the kids need to define themselves by the superficial whims of bullies but rather that they may need to learn to be adaptable to their environment.

In a potential bullying environment, some parents may need to help their children discern what's in and what's not. If everyone in the school values certain clothing labels and looks down on the kids who are wearing clothes from Penneys, then the parents may need to steer their less socially savvy kid towards these labels. Of course some parents won't be able to afford to keep up with expensive styles that teenagers prefer; however, depending on the context, it might be worthwhile for the parent to forego other luxuries in order to buy one or two items each year so the teenager can keep their head above water when they are with their judgemental peers. I'm aware that many parents will believe they are selling out by making their child fit in and this might be true. However, if the environment is vicious then it is probably worth it. If the environment is supportive then your child should be safe to wear whatever they choose. Although individuality is important, any last vestige of individuality will be wiped out if they are bullied and so it might be better to weigh up the choice between keeping individuality in a difficult environment versus being bullied in a difficult environment. Of course the ideal solution is to put the child in a more tolerant environment in the first place!

> *'I trace my alcoholism back to when I was bullied in first year in secondary school. I will never forget how I felt in English class when the teacher asked John O'Connor to read out his story. Halfway through the story, the horrifying realisation dawned upon me that the entire story was actually about me. Everyone was sniggering and tittering in the classroom and I literally wanted to die. The story was all about a boy who was gay but he pretended not to be. Everyone saw through him but he didn't know it. I'll never forget the moment that I realised the story was about me. I went hot and then I went cold. I was bent over my desk, frozen to the spot. The girls were all giggling. I felt so exposed and vulnerable, it's hard to describe. The teacher didn't really know how to handle it — in hindsight he should have simply stopped the story as soon as he realised what was happening but instead he focused on stopping the other kids throwing things at me and giggling and nudging me — which was even more humiliating for me.'*
>
> *Kevin, 28*

In certain situations, parents are better able to 'read' the social moves. If this is the case, the parent needs to teach their child these social codes. Sometimes parents might also need to teach their children other social subtleties such as not to boast, to recognise the 'stop signals', not to keep repeating a joke if no one laughs and other little tendencies their child might have that won't help them. It can also be helpful if the parent can teach their child to connect with themselves on an authentic level so that they can learn to be themselves without coming across as a faker. No one is more highly tuned to phoniness than teenagers.

Parents can help their kids to box clever: they can keep their individuality at home, they can express themselves with creative writing or music, but at the same time they needn't open themselves to abuse by rattling the cage of the potential bullies. These are hard truths but bullying is a very hard situation. Viktor Frankl, in his seminal book about how he survived the concentration camps during World War II, *Man's Search for Meaning*, described how he retained some semblance of control over his diabolical situation by identifying a purpose in life to feel positively about, and then imagining that outcome. For example, if your child can imagine one day living a happier life when they go to college, with friends and acceptance, then they can more readily accept their current circumstances.

Preparing wisely

Parents who wish to raise children who can handle our culture need to take a big step back from their family and assess calmly and forensically the following questions. This emotional insight then needs to be fed to your child so that they become more self-aware and better equipped to handle the more difficult aspects of their culture.

What are the traits that drive your children? Are they friendly? Critical? Witty? Eager to please? Slow to warm up?

What are the traits they possess that will help them in this world? Could their sensitivity give them the opportunity to quickly understand the bullying dynamic? Could they use their sense of humour to their advantage?

What do they find difficult about their environment (e.g. school, social media, boys)? Is the social interaction the most difficult aspect? Are they more immature than other kids their age? Does their lack of interest in sport go against them?

How do your kids respond to attack? Do they choose fight, flight, freeze or appease? Does it work out for them? What could they do (there is no point in giving them advice that they just couldn't do) that would be even a tiny bit more helpful?

The school environment

The real solution to social difficulties can often be to focus on the environment rather than the bullies, because, within the right environment, potential bullies won't become bullies (they may instead become powerful and motivated leaders or else their destructive tendencies may be channelled in other more creative ways). Part of the role of the principal and the teacher is to create a bully-resistant environment that doesn't allow this behaviour to flourish. The only problem with this is that it's not the main role of any school to prevent bullying. Further, the education system itself is a classically pro-bullying environment insofar as it has a competitive and hierarchical system with students ultimately competing with each other for places in their third-level course of choice. The psychology of schools and universities banks on the fact that everyone has something to prove. The education system in its current state fosters the culture of constant achievement and, therefore, relentless stress and insecurity.

Teachers are paid to teach their students, not to prevent bullying from taking place, and although they might preach about the evils of bullying and they might support anti-bullying initiatives, if we are to stamp it out a good deal more sustained effort and focus is required from schools, families and the entire community.

Some proactive teachers find it helpful to use the classroom environment to focus on character and leadership traits as a way of guiding children's choices instead of rules. They can do this through the use of punitive writing assignments on themes such as loyalty, compassion, kindness or moral courage so that when a child behaves badly they have to write on a topic that forces them to think about their actions in terms of this theme.

Teachers can create an 'upstanding' environment by running art projects and history projects based upon key moments in history such as the Civil Rights Movement. If the teacher chooses certain aspects of history to show how a small number of people can make a difference, the lessons can have a profound impact on key potential upstanders in the classroom – and a classroom only needs a couple of effective upstanders to change the culture of bystanding.

Teachers pitting students against each other in a bid to achieve better results is fraught with tension and leads to a bullying atmosphere. The school environment can help by fostering group cohesion within the school, a kind of 'we're all in this together' atmosphere about exams and getting into college. St Columb's in Derry (whose notable alumni include Seamus Heaney,

Brian Friel, John Hume, Paul Brady and Phil Coulter) fostered this spirit by giving a day off to the whole school whenever a student won a prestigious university scholarship. Teachers can also create an anti-bullying environment by being careful about the tone they set in the classroom. If the tone is insecure, competitive and strictly hierarchical, the class culture can easily turn towards bullying, and it is the role of the teacher to create a safe and encouraging place for children to thrive and flourish – despite our nasty system of education!

Handling difference

If a child feels threatened by the arrival of someone 'different' into their social sphere, the child can react by bullying or excluding this person, not only because they wish to protect the purity of the group, but also because the potential bully doesn't understand their complicated and emotional reaction to the new person; for example, when a powerful but morally unengaged child is confronted with somebody who appears to have a whole slew of complicated challenges such as special needs or a difficult family background.

Children can be overwhelmed by their feelings of horror, survivor guilt and genuine relief that they don't have these challenges. These potential bullies are often motivated by their instinctive desire to avoid difficult emotions and their attempts to control the uncontrollable. So they might mindlessly exclude a person who is 'different' simply because they are repelled by their difference. While this may all be understandable, it is a pretty horrible experience for the new person to be bullied or excluded simply because they are different. A culture of education, tolerance, compassion and empathy is needed to ensure that newness and difference is handled appropriately. Teachers can create this culture within the classroom simply by focusing upon these subjects in the literature students read, the songs they sing, the important figures they read about and the history they learn.

The importance of acceptance

The gift of self-acceptance and other acceptance is perhaps one of the most powerful gifts you can give your child. Parents and teachers can lead the way with regular discussions about how difference can be great and how it can be a difficult but worthwhile mantle to bear — for example, Lady Gaga and Stephen Hawking are very different compared to their peers.

A narrow-minded or bigoted attitude isn't acceptable, but it is unfortunately very common and the more your child learns about different people's attitudes, the more your child will build and develop their emotional intelligence, their self-acceptance and other acceptance.

If your child is in some way different it is important for you to teach your child about people's uneducated attitude to difference. It can take some time for a child to learn to love their difference but in the meantime parents can read appropriate children's books with their younger children to support their child's emotional insight, and watch movies with their older children (see the resources at the back of this book). The parent can also teach the child that society hasn't quite evolved sufficiently to allow people who are different to live happily in our midst — that often ignorant people will attack difference and this, sadly, is an experience that they should both anticipate and learn how to handle.

There is strength in being different and, with some careful encouragement and nurturing, your child's difference might be the key element that contributes to your child one day becoming a compassionate, considerate and powerful adult.

Cohesion and competitiveness

The cohesiveness of the group is a significant factor that influences whether bullying is allowed to continue. As we saw with Denmark in the previous chapter, where the Jewish Danes were considered part of the Danish community, the more cohesive the group, the more likely the bystanders will engage morally with any given situation. Rather than looking over their shoulder and waiting to be stabbed in the back by their frenemies, a cohesive group has the strength and the support of the group. This is where the school environment really matters – if the environment is cohesive and has a culture where upstanding is recognised and supported, then people are much more likely to protect the vulnerable. However, when the group is insecure or incohesive it is much more difficult to be strong enough to stand out. Members of an incohesive group are more likely to aggressively try to establish a pecking order and so they can become hyper-focused on throwing out any dubious members of the group. The weaker members of the herd are so bent on strengthening their group (and thereby strengthening themselves) they can be ruthless in their tendency to attack others.

Adults often forget how desperate children are to blend in with the crowd. Even the kids who stand out because of extraordinary achievements tend to be embarrassed by standing out – most kids spend all their waking hours making sure that they are part of the crowd, and if they're not, are desperately trying to get in with a crowd. And when you're a teenager living on the outskirts of the 'in-crowd', always aware that one false move could relegate you to 'loner' status, this is an emotionally fraught situation.

Adults loudly wagging their fingers and telling their kids to stand up for anyone who is being bullied are often missing the point. The situation is so much more complicated than that and not many of us will willingly put our heads into the lion's mouth on purpose. Teenagers inhabit a virtual world where 'friends' are counted obsessively and changing your profile picture is a major life event. The social world that teenagers live by today is complex, ruthless, subtle and incredibly conscious of social standing. Adults do their children a disservice by jumping in with bland and insensitive advice that denies the complexity of the situation.

Teenagers, when they aren't filled with fear, can lack confidence in their ability to make a difference in any given situation – they tell themselves they don't know how to make it stop. Just like watching a car crash or a horrible fight outside the chipper on a Saturday night, many of us freeze in the face of horror. This is all the more true for teenagers and children who have little knowledge about how to appropriately handle such behaviour. The ambiguity of any complex bullying situation inhibits the kids from acting – they often can't quite figure out who is to blame and what should be done. If the group is insecure, the entire situation gives them a pain in the brain and so, out of frustration and helplessness, they simply turn away.

Group identity

Avid football fans often particularly enjoy the sense of belonging that 'their' team provides – all you have to do is attend any football match to see a group's identity in action. But why are some people happy to go for a burger and go home after the match while others feel the need to be caught up in the groundswell of mob mentality? Why do fans set cars on fire after they lose, and even after they *win*, a game of football?

Individually, these people are often very nice and even sweet, but as a group they can become violent oiks. As we have seen in the previous chapter, research on the science of mob behaviour shows us that individuals can 'lose touch' with their own morality when they are in a group. The group can create a bullying environment – and this environment is susceptible to change.

When we look at the recent World Cup in France in 2016 we can soon see how each mob creates its own identity. The Irish fans became proud that they had the moniker 'the best fans in the world' and so, to further identify with this reputation, they began doing extraordinarily random acts of kindness around France during the World Cup, such as changing an old French couple's car tyre, tidying up after a raucous night of drinking and even singing a baby to sleep!

Meanwhile the English and Russian fans self-identified as being the hardest fans in the world. The Russian fans were described as savage and coordinated. They disguised themselves as English fans and equipped themselves with gum shields and telescopic truncheons. This military approach meant that they viewed their identity as warlike, where the fans – never mind the football teams – would either win or lose. Previously, English fans were notorious around the world for their rioting and fighting and evidently the Russian fans became determined to steal this dubious title from them by 'beating' them.

But, thankfully, the mentality of the mob can change (as can the school environment). When the Irish fans met the English fans in Montmartre, the English fans behaved very differently from how they behaved with the Russians. The Irish fans weren't trying to 'beat' the English fans with violence, rather they immediately set about securing their identity as the 'friendliest' fans and began slagging the English with chants of 'Please don't start a riot'. The English fans responded with 'You're just an English B team'. It was all very good-natured and when the Irish began to chant, 'Someone call the Russians' the slagging was accepted as all in good fun. Because one of the groups had no interest at all in being violent, the other group fell in with the new competition to see which fans were the funniest, just as a competitive school can become a school that is competitive about how kind and inclusive it is.

Being part of a group leads most of us to heightened emotional states. This is why many people like going to music concerts – it's seldom for the sound quality, but rather for the large emotional connection with others who appreciate the same music. These emotional states can be positive as well as negative. Rage, terror, bliss, exhilaration – all of these emotional states can be harnessed into the one group. So long as the emotional state is a positive one, it is harmless enough, but when the emotional state is a negative one it becomes more dangerous. And so, if a school environment has a very competitive atmosphere, then the most productive response is to move the competition towards charity and acts of kindness. Equally, if a school is boring and unchallenging, ringleaders can turn to bullying as a form of entertainment and so the indolent atmosphere should be changed to a more satisfyingly productive environment.

The perfect bullying environment

When we examine the harsh and doctrinaire environment of an old-fashioned boarding school, we soon see how the school environment can have a profound impact. Old-fashioned private boarding schools were often a Petri dish for creating bullies. Many of these schools regularly dished out collective punishment as a disciplinary measure. This authoritarian approach that punished the whole class rather than the one or two guilty students bred anger and isolation. Back in the day, there was little emphasis on gentleness, kindness or compassion and instead strength and power were often glorified. Consequently certain personalities thrived in these circumstances while other, gentler personalities – like Prince Charles, for example – suffered tremendously. To this day, certain private schools' over-the-top emphasis on achievement, social status and power can nurture a bullying atmosphere. Competition is often actively encouraged in private schools as these schools need to show fee-paying parents that attending their private school is an investment worth spending money on and so they like to demonstrate achievement and performance. Thankfully, many private schools today focus their competitiveness on more altruistic concerns.

Hazing is the ritualistic practice of initiating novices into the school culture that was very common in boarding schools and is still prevalent in some schools today. Hazing primarily serves to ensure that everyone knows their place. This creates a strict hierarchy that relies on bullying as a way to ensure that the pecking order is maintained. The targets of the bullying can then console themselves that one day they will be in the upper echelons of the school and they, in turn, will have the chance to mete out nasty punishments to those younger and smaller than themselves. And they often do.

Although such behaviour in schools isn't openly tolerated, nevertheless, many adults are of the misguided opinion that this behaviour is part of the rough and tumble of childhood and that it toughens us up. It isn't, though, and it doesn't.

'I've often wondered which was worse; being bullied or feeling isolated by my former friends, by the teachers and by my parents who all stood back and allowed the bullies to ruin my life. It has changed my entire worldview. It makes me sound like a psycho but I can actually understand why some bullied kids go ballistic and shoot up the whole school. There needs to be a process to painlessly file complaints and to automatically escalate resolution after a certain threshold is reached. Unless children have the opportunity to complain without exposing themselves to further harm, bullying will continue.'

John, 42

Being your child's advocate

It is remarkable to me, as a psychotherapist, how many clients tell me that they just need to toughen up and learn to endure whatever it is that is causing them distress. I generally point out to them that they have been saying this to themselves for many years – sometimes for as much as fifty, sixty or even seventy years – and they still haven't learned to toughen up and so perhaps a more effective and courageous response would be to try another approach. Indeed, in many ways, it is often braver to admit to yourself that an approach isn't working; sometimes it is braver to be gentle and tender. Similarly, parents should refrain from asking their children to 'toughen up' and instead help them to help themselves.

As a novice therapist, I was given this poem by my friend and teacher Fiona Hoban, and I believe it powerfully reminds us how to help our children without treading upon them:

If you are going to help me ...

Please be patient while I decide if I can trust you.

Let me tell my story. The whole story, in my own way.

Please accept that whatever I have done and whatever I may do

are my choices and seem right to me at the time.

I am not just a person. I am this person; unique, not the same as you or anyone else you've known.

Don't judge me as bad or good. I am who I am and that is all.

Do not assume that your knowledge about me is more accurate than mine.

You only know what I have told you. That is only part of me.

Do not think that you know what I should do – you don't.

I may be confused, but I am still the expert about me.

Do not place me in a position of living up to your expectations. I have enough trouble with mine.

Hear my feelings – not just my words. Accept them; don't try to fix me.

Do not try to save me.

I can do that myself.

I knew enough to ask for help.

Help me help myself.

— **Unknown**

The challenges that parents will face from the school are numerous. First, schools often minimise and deny that bullying is taking place; second, schools operate on a strict budget and would rather not spend money on extra-curricular initiatives such as anti-bullying programmes; and third, schools are supposed to be focused on education, and students' mental well-being is beyond many teachers' training. Nevertheless, it's the squeaky wheel that gets the oil and, as your child's advocate, it might be necessary for you to speak up and continue to speak up if you are to ensure that your child's school is adequately caring for and protecting your child.

Many parents of children who have been bullied regret having so much respect for the authority of the school. In hindsight, they feel that the school made them feel as though it was their child's fault that they were bullied and they allowed the school to refuse to address the issue. It is up to the parent to figure out the appropriate action when the school is dismissive – see more about unhelpful schools in Chapter 8.

'When my child was bullied in first year in secondary school, I'm afraid I did everything wrong. We're a quiet family and so when Laura came home from school with stories about the notorious Allie and her rough mates annoying her I kept urging Laura to stay away from them. That was my first mistake — it was naive to think that my thirteen-year-old kid had the capacity to avoid the bullies; they were in her class — how did I think she was going to avoid them?! Laura was quiet as a mouse, she had a mild disposition and, as she had moved from a small country school to a huge secondary school she hadn't made enough friends to have any support — looking back she was ripe to be bullied.

In hindsight I think I should have focused on helping Laura to find a social circle where she felt comfortable. She found it difficult socially in those initial weeks and months of secondary school and I should've been more supportive and involved before things got out of control.

I think Laura was targeted because she was unusually tall for her age — such a silly thing, but looks are everything at that age — and because she was quiet and passive. When the bullies began calling her 'Laura the Loner'. I told her to laugh it off, to ignore them. That was my second mistake — I now know I should've gone straight into the school at that point and raised hell — insisted anti-bullying initiatives be brought in so that the bystanders' consciences were pricked and insisted that each bully got spoken to and warned off.

Unbeknownst to me the bullies upped the ante and started to stalk Laura outside of school hours, on social media and on her mobile. Laura became withdrawn and used to complain all the time about feeling sick. In my heart of hearts, I knew that she had problems at school but I hate conflict myself and I hoped that these were just teething problems as she settled into the new school. I'm not socially confident and this weakness impacted Laura's life at this crucial time.

The problem for Laura was that by December of first year, it was social suicide to be friendly with 'the loner'. There were some girls who would visit her after school but Laura said they kept their distance during school hours. One day, after Laura had pulled yet another sickie, she told me that she ate her lunch in a different toilet cubicle every day. She killed time at her locker during the short break. She used to eat very quietly for fear of being caught and ridiculed by her schoolmates. She had to change cubicles because she feared that she would be found out. I was devastated. I have always had difficulty making friends myself and I had dearly hoped that my daughter would be able to have the fun-filled teenage years that I had missed out on myself.

My husband was pretty useless — he just kept saying 'girls are such bitches' without coming up with any solutions. Laura was mortified — she felt like a failure and a reject. And I was completely out of my comfort zone. I am one of nature's people-pleasers. I don't like making waves — indeed I had never complained about anything in my life before Laura was bullied. Consequently, when I first tried to address the situation with the school I was too polite and timid. The school's response was polished and professional — we don't allow bullying here so don't worry, this will be handled immediately.'

It wasn't.

The bullies continued to stalk Laura in the school, on the bus, on her phone, on social media. More precious time was wasted feebly hoping things would 'settle'. She became more and more miserable. She hated school and her grades slipped.

I contacted the school again and this time I burst into tears. They arranged for me to go in to the school — now I know I should've insisted on a face-to-face meeting the first time around. I went in and the principal and the deputy principal met me and assured me that they would haul in the bullies one by one and sort them out effectively.

The feelings of helplessness and powerlessness almost defeated me a few weeks later when I looked at Laura's Instagram account and realised that the bullying was still going on. I am still shocked at the murderous rage that almost overtook me when I saw those nasty images about 'Laura the Loner' on her page. I could have happily strangled the lot of them had I met them that night.

Still the bullying continued, still the school told us that they were handling it, and still Laura was eating her lunch in the toilets.

The school was useless, I was useless and my husband was useless — and Laura bore the brunt of all this. Eventually, after the end of a terrible, terrible year, we moved Laura to another school. She is doing OK now but she has lost her sense of trust in the world. She is secretive and embittered and doesn't really trust anyone any more. The merry little girl who used to laugh so easily has gone and in her place is a sad and insecure, miserable girl.'

Eileen, 47

Sadly, Eileen's reaction to her daughter's situation and the school's ineffective response to her complaints are all too familiar. Many of the clients I meet have experienced bullying over an extended period of time with the schools continuing to reassure the parents that they were dealing with it, when they weren't really. However, there are certain lessons we can take away from this common story.

If you have a quiet, passive child who is moving into a new environment, extra care might need to be taken so that your child has more support than usual, especially if they have anything at all about them that could be considered 'unusual' by other teens or tweens – there is no one as freakishly conforming as a young teenager! This might mean attending certain activities that will help your child socialise more easily, or reigniting an old friendship or perhaps creating a space for your child and you to chat alone regularly – maybe go for a hot chocolate every Friday or something similar – so that any worries can be aired and dealt with as soon as they arise.

Another lesson to learn from this story is that asking a quiet and passive child to 'laugh away' insults is insensitive and inappropriate. If the child was able to easily laugh away their concerns, they'd be doing it without your prompting; similarly, advising your child to 'stand up to them' is inappropriate if the whole point is that they don't feel able to!

The parent needs to learn how to handle the school authorities effectively and refuse to be waved away. You may have to enlist others to act as an advocate if you aren't coping well with the school. Parents also need to be willing to confront their own weaknesses so that they can properly help their children. This might entail seeking counselling or further support if needs be.

Phoebe Prince was born in England in 1994 and her family moved to Co. Clare when she was two years old. In 2009, Phoebe moved with her mother and four siblings to the US, but within six months of the big move Phoebe had died by suicide. Her parents chose to bury her in Ireland.

Phoebe was involved in bullying when she was in school in Co. Limerick before she moved to the US. Phoebe was already troubled at this stage and she was self-harming. She was among the leaders of an online bullying campaign against a Pakistani girl with whom Phoebe had originally been good friends. Phoebe fell out with her erstwhile friend over a boy and called her a 'Paki Whore' and other nasty names. As a direct result of the bullying, the girl was removed from the school by her parents. Phoebe subsequently wrote a letter of apology which was praised by the victim's mother.

When Phoebe moved to the US she was initially well liked among her schoolmates. She was an attractive and personable girl, but she had a habit of targeting boys who were already involved with other girls.

Phoebe seemed to have been a complex and unhappy girl. Her family was split and her much-adored father was living back in Co. Clare while she was in the US. Phoebe had a history of self-harming and her aunt had warned the school authorities in the US that Phoebe was susceptible to problems such as bullying.

In her short time in the US, Phoebe confessed to different boys that she was cutting herself. Each individual boy she told was often sympathetic but they didn't have the emotional intelligence or maturity to be able to handle the situation.

Phoebe's unhappiness was well known to the school administration in the US but they didn't act effectively. Prior to her death Phoebe's mother had spoken to at least two staff members and Phoebe had also spoken to the school's social worker who knew that Phoebe was self-harming.

On the day of her suicide Phoebe had told a boy that she should probably 'od' (overdose). The boy was kind but he didn't know what to do. That day she was taunted as an 'Irish whore' (poignantly reminiscent of the names she had called the girl in Co. Limerick) by another girl and a can was thrown at her. Phoebe went home and hung herself. She was just fifteen years old and her body was discovered by her 12-year-old sister. Following Phoebe's death, the six teenagers who were accused of bullying Phoebe were themselves subjected to bullying and death threats, and Phoebe's father expressed concern regarding their treatment by the public.

The litany of missed opportunities that characterise Phoebe Prince's life shows us just how woeful many people are when dealing with problems in adolescence. In Phoebe's first second-level school her bullying didn't seem to have been well handled as the target felt compelled to leave the school. In her school in the US the 'bitch fights' that Phoebe was often involved in were a common feature of school life and so a blind eye was often turned. The bullying culture that was so rampant in Phoebe's troubled life was pretty much dismissed as typical 'girl drama', but her tragic end shows us how troubling behaviour, if not handled properly, can sometimes be fatal. More than anything, Phoebe was clearly a girl who needed extra emotional support and her family and school, although aware of her troubles, for some reason weren't able to provide adequate support for her. Sadly, Phoebe mostly turned to boys in her school, instead of concerned adults, for emotional support and these boys weren't emotionally equipped to deal with this. Perhaps if Phoebe had been provided with more appropriate support she wouldn't have felt the need to end her life in such a tragic way.

Parents set the tone for their children's childhood. If the parent can manage to set a tone that shows strength when they feel attacked, their children can learn to model this behaviour. This assertiveness might come easily for some children in the family while others may not find being assertive so easy. However, just as you could if your child had dyslexia or dyscalculia, you can help them overcome their lack of assertiveness by providing extra support.

Parents through their actions can also show their child how to respond appropriately within the school setting. For example, if your child tells you about a child who is being bullied, you might contact the school, if appropriate, and then let your child know that you have taken action in terms of the objectionable behaviour.

If nothing changes then you can complain about the bullying again – and again, and again. Even if the school is dismissive and doesn't listen to your complaints, you can be a force for good by contacting the parents of a child who is being bullied and showing your solidarity with them. Your child, in turn, can learn to stand shoulder to shoulder with the target of the bullying by being kind to them and looking out for them.

What you can do

The bullying environment is one of the elements of any bullying situation that can be sorted out comprehensively. Parents can become actively involved in creating an anti-bullying environment in a school, but some parents will need to leave their comfort zone in order to carry this out. Most of us say that we'd gladly take a bullet for our children; in this case, instead of taking a bullet, passive, shy and conforming parents may have to speak out and be counted.

Parents of children who have been targeted can find it beneficial to join the parents' committee and subsequently persuade the committee to run specific anti-bullying programmes that are available. If the school pleads poverty then you might need to begin a fundraising initiative to pay for such a programme – and you can start the whole thing off with a generous donation from yourself. Parents can also organise other initiatives to help stamp out bullying in the schools and ensure that further anti-bullying measures are carried out. Speakers can be invited to speak to parents and children at different times. Buddy benches, bully boxes, anti-bullying ambassadors, a culture of kindness and other workable initiatives can also be integrated within the school system (see Chapter 8).

Of course, many parents who are feeling completely overwhelmed by their child's experience of bullying will not feel able to join the parents' committee as they will view the school establishment as the enemy. If this is really the case, then perhaps it is time for your child to move schools. However, if you have any energy left at all to fight for your child, then you should begin by turning up at the principal's office, the year head's office and the parents' committee and forcefully insisting that specific anti-bullying measures are brought into the school. As the author and anthropologist Margaret Mead said, 'Never doubt that a small group of thoughtful, committed citizens can change the world; indeed, it's the only thing that ever has.'

7

Cyberbullying
Trolls, hate mail and sextortion

'Don't be mean behind your screen.'

Anti-bullying Facebook page

Bullying has taken a dark turn and, more than anything else, it is cyberbullying that seems to strike terror in the hearts of parents these days. Most parents have experienced bullying as a child, either as a target, a bystander or a bully and, although we loathe it, we can, on some level, understand it. But the cruel, weird, relentless nature of cyberbullying unnerves parents more because many of us can't imagine what it must feel like to be ostracised, insulted or publicly humiliated on social media. Added to that, the belief that these posts can never be deleted tends to completely overwhelm parents.

We tell our kids never to post pictures of themselves online, but posting pictures has become so normalised that this is like asking kids not to use Google or not to use social media. Anyway, many parents incessantly ask their young kids to pose for cute pictures and so it is often parents who start the habit. It's a bit much to then ask these cute-kids-turned-teenagers to suddenly stop posing and posting. It's unlikely that teenagers will listen to advice not to post photos – rather they will just think the advice is out of date. It is worth repeating: teenagers will definitely post photos of themselves. This phenomenon is just too widespread to stop – it is more relevant to ensure they have enough social nous to discriminate between a safe pic and a potentially embarrassing pic.

Kids communicate in images these days. They don't post 'I'm at the cinema' – they post a picture of the cinema; they don't post that they are enjoying a hot chocolate with pals – they post a picture of smiling faces with hot chocolate in the centre. The first foray into flirting is via social media these days – it's easier for a tween or teenager to flirt with a suggestive message that has been perfectly constructed with the help of five pals than to try to spontaneously flirt 'irl'. The problem with this is that the most current research suggests that the more social networking a preteen does, the more socially nervous they become. [36]

Thankfully, with the many progressive initiatives available, it is now eminently possible to sort out bullying in schools. Unfortunately bullying often shifts from the school towards a more ungovernable cloud in the cyber sky. Certain tech companies are trying, in their way, to control the more negative aspects of social media but, as Dave Willner, the former head of the Hate and Harassment team at Facebook, says, 'Bullying is hard. It's slippery to define, and it's even harder when it's writing instead of speech. Tone of voice disappears.'[37] The prevailing wisdom is that the online content moderation system is broken and relying on a broken system to protect your child from abuse is misguided and foolhardy. There are certain procedures available on social media to block someone from your account, to complain about a page and to get a post or a page deleted, but these are often slow, not in any way foolproof, and many, many people fall through the cracks.

Keyboard warriors

It is notable that the main impulse driving most cyberbullying appears to be to 'bring people down'. Successful people, beautiful people and celebrities are ripped up by bitter keyboard warriors who make themselves feel better by making other people feel worse. Similarly, in the school environment, it is often the young and beautiful girls who are vulnerable to being targeted by online bullies. It is not only their beauty that makes them vulnerable to being bullied – although this can provoke envy and vindictiveness. But if they are beautiful as well as gentle, passive, vulnerable or provocative then this combination makes bullying much more likely to happen.

Beautiful girls' lives can be ripped apart by angry boys who can't have them and by jealous girls who know they can never hope to be as alluring. As the French writer André Breton wrote of the Salem witch trials, 'At the word witch, we imagine the horrible old crones from Macbeth. But the cruel trials witches suffered teach us the opposite. Many perished precisely because they were young and beautiful.'

If we look at the Salem Witch Trials, the Ku Klux Klan and the horrors of World War II, we soon see how ordinary, hitherto decent people can become infected by other people's cruelty. We need to be watchful of the dark side of human nature that is prone to destroying others to feel superior. Online, where similarly minded individuals are more liable to meet, and where emotions and impulsivity run high, the risk of mass hysteria appears to be more common. (Parents of teenage girls should perhaps note that mass hysteria is most common among groups of females who share common spaces for long periods of time.)

'When I was 15 I fell madly in love with Stephen. He was the coolest guy in our year. All the girls fancied him and he didn't seem to let it go to his head — he seemed to genuinely like girls. One day Stephen stopped me at my locker and asked me to meet him after school. I was on cloud nine; I thought it was the best day of my life.

We became boyfriend and girlfriend and I thought life couldn't get any better. We used to FaceTime each other last thing at night to say good night and of course I always made sure I looked good for our FaceTime. Stephen always showered me with such lovely compliments and so, as time went on, I put ever more effort into my outfits for our FaceTime. I lapped up all the compliments and our FaceTime became more intimate.

Stephen used to beg me for some pictures; he always told me how beautiful I looked. Before Stephen, no one had ever told me I was pretty let alone beautiful. Every single day he would ask me to send him a picture and I often did — funny ones and silly ones — but eventually the constant requests wore me down and the pictures I sent became more and more suggestive; first, of me wearing revealing tops, then a quick flirtatious glimpse here and there and eventually no top at all.

A year or so later we broke up because Stephen became jealous and possessive. I thought the whole thing was done and dusted and it never even entered my head that I could be a victim of 'revenge porn' until I saw my photos on social media.

Stephen pretended that I was sending him nude pictures to get him back — this was because I had broken up with him and he felt humiliated. The comments underneath my pictures are forever burned on my brain; apparently I was a 'desperate slut' and a 'skanky whore that would give you warts'. These were comments from horrible little boys from the year below me who had probably never even been kissed. When people that I actually knew and liked made nasty comments I was devastated.

I couldn't bring myself to tell my parents — how do you tell your parents that your bare breasts are all over social media and everyone thinks you are a skanky slut? I did tell my parents that I was being bullied but when they complained to the school of course the teachers knew nothing about it.

I convinced my mother to let me change school but the images followed me. I started self-harming. I hated myself for being such a fool and I hated myself because everyone else did. One particularly horrible day a nasty little prick from my new school posted a 'hilarious video' that supposedly showed me being screwed by dogs. Of course the video wasn't true but the rumour mill rushed around the school that I did it with dogs. Suddenly everyone was whistling at me as if I was a dog.

The mixture of rage and humiliation spurred me to drink a bottle of vodka and slash my wrists. To this day, I'm not sure if I wanted to kill myself or if I just wanted to hurt myself and make everyone pay for their horrible comments. After my suicide attempt my mother found me a good therapist and, although we've had a few false starts, we are now getting on really well and I feel a glimmer of hope about my future. I'm not so disturbed by pictures of me online — as far I'm concerned, anyone who searches for these pictures and judges me on them are probably not the sort of person I would respect.'

Amy, 18

Social media is built upon the premise of a pyramid scheme of agreement – you 'like' my picture and then I'm more likely to 'like' yours. This 'mutual approval machine' means that we surround ourselves with people who approve of our way of thinking. If someone gets in the way of this cosy consensus we tend to screen them out. Many keyboard warriors pride themselves on their political righteousness and they are prepared to go to almost any lengths to convince others of it too; indeed, the majority of trolls on social media appear to be from the highly sensitive liberal classes.

As Jon Ronson, author of the polemical *So You've Been Publicly Shamed*, said in his TED talk:

> *In the early days of Twitter, it was like a place of radical de-shaming. People would admit shameful secrets about themselves, and other people would say, 'Oh my God, I'm exactly the same.' Voiceless people realized that they had a voice, and it was powerful and eloquent. If a newspaper ran some racist or homophobic column, we realized we could do something about it. We could get them. We could hit them with a weapon that we understood but they didn't – a social media shaming. Advertisers would withdraw their advertising. When powerful people misused their privilege, we were going to get them. This was like the democratization of justice. Hierarchies were being levelled out. We were going to do things better.*[38]

This was the great premise of social media – the voiceless people suddenly had a voice. In 2010, when Lola the cat was saved after being dumped in a wheelie bin, social media cheered with delight. The people had power! We could make the world a better place with our moral righteousness!

Those were heady days, but unfortunately, things didn't stay like that. The keyboard warriors were corrupted by power, and now that the people had a powerful voice, they often acted like the East German Stasi: ever-vigilant and ready to persecute and torture anyone who was so foolish as to make a slightly inappropriate comment.

In his TED talk and also in his book, Jon Ronson explores the extraordinary story of Justine Sacco. Justine Sacco was an ordinary working woman from New York with a measly 170 Twitter followers when she tweeted a poorly thought-out joke. It wasn't a good joke and it seemed a bit inappropriate, although it turned out that she was clumsily trying to make a point about the way Americans can flaunt their privilege. The now-infamous joke ran like this: 'Going to Africa. Hope I don't get AIDS. Just kidding. I'm white!'

She pressed send, got on the plane and turned off her phone. Eleven hours later, when she turned on her phone as the plane was taxiing onto the runway in Cape Town, she was the worldwide number one trending topic on Twitter. This vague, ill-considered joke was about to ruin her life. Initially, the philanthropists criticised her words, calling it a 'disgusting, racist tweet', but it soon got darker with tweets like 'Everyone go report this cunt @JustineSacco', 'Good luck with the job hunt in the new year. #GettingFired' and '@JustineSacco last tweet of your career #SorryNotSorry'. Suddenly thousands of people from around the world decided it was their moral duty that day to be part of a campaign to get this woman fired. Of course the trolls waded in with their tuppence worth, 'I'm actually kind of hoping Justine Sacco gets aids?' and 'Somebody HIV-positive should rape this bitch and then we'll find out if her skin color protects her from AIDS.' And so, that night, the politically correct philanthropists were in bed with the demented loons who recommended that we 'rape this bitch'.

As Jon Ronson said:

> *A lot of companies were making good money that night. You know, Justine's name was normally Googled 40 times a month. That month, between December the 20th and the end of December, her name was Googled 1,220,000 times. And one Internet economist told me that that meant that Google made somewhere between 120,000 dollars and 468,000 dollars from Justine's annihilation, whereas those of us doing the actual shaming – we got nothing. We were like unpaid shaming interns for Google.*[39]

Someone worked out exactly which plane she was on and suddenly the whole of the Twitterati waited with bated breath, using the hashtag #HasJustineLandedYet, as Justine got off the flight and turned on her phone. A picture was taken of her reading her phone in the airport while social media rocked with joy as they ruined the life of an ordinary woman who made a bad joke.

The casual cruelty evident on social media is shocking. The keyboard warriors who can be quite likeable in person can be catty, reactionary bigots online. Sadly, whenever someone becomes publicly vulnerable, a contest to see who can be the wittiest person online often begins. It doesn't matter how cruel or irrelevant the comment is – the funniest comment wins the game. It is an unforgiving and nasty phenomenon. It is also notably misogynistic and racist.

The *Guardian* newspaper researched the online harassment of its own writers and discovered that eight out of ten contributors who receive the most online abuse are women – five white and three non-white – and the other two were black men. Female *Guardian* writers who wrote about rape and feminism received the most abuse. Not only that, but abuse towards women is more vicious and more personal – as Ronson pointed out, 'When a man is shamed, it's usually, "I'm going to get you fired." When a woman is shamed it's, "I'm going to rape you and get you fired."'

Kara Kowalski from West Virginia in the US was a popular girl in her school. She had been crowned 'Queen of Charm' and was on the cheerleading squad. One fine day when Kara was seventeen years old, she decided to create a page on social media called 'S.A.S.H' which, it later emerged, stood for 'Students Against Shay's Herpes'. Shay was the name of a girl in Kara's school. The subheading on the page was 'No, No Herpes, We Don't Want No Herpes.' After inviting about 100 people to join the page, about two dozen teenagers accepted Kara's invitation. One classmate, Ray, posted a photo of himself with another boy holding their noses, with a sign that read 'Shay has herpes'. Kara commented 'You are so funny'. Ray added pictures of Shay; in one he drew red dots on her face and added a sign in front of her pelvis reading 'Warning: Enter at your own risk.' Another picture was captioned 'Portrait of a whore'.

We can try for a moment to imagine how Shay might have felt when she spoke to her family about this but most of us simply can't make that leap: it is just too far from our own experience. Shay's father called Ray to express his fury. Ray called Kara to ask her to take the page down. Kara tried to take the page down but couldn't figure out how.

The next morning, Shay and her parents visited the school principal and showed her the 'S.A.S.H' page. Understandably,

Shay skipped classes that day. The principal suspended Kara for ten days but when Kara's parents protested, the suspension was cut in half. Kara was kicked off the cheerleading squad and stripped of the privilege of crowning the school's next 'Queen of Charm'.

Kara's parents believed this was inappropriate and, in a shocking display of arrogant self-righteousness, sued the school, arguing that the suspension violated her right to free speech. When she lost her case they appealed to the Supreme Court.

Kara's case was denied an appeal.

Hate mail

Hate mail isn't new; we have all heard of the poison-pen letter and the obscene phone call. But now, with the ease of access and effortless anonymity that is provided by our computers, hate mail has perhaps taken on a life of its own. It is just so much easier to fire off a crazy, hate-filled post to someone who has annoyed you than to go to the trouble of writing a letter, disguising your identity and handwriting and then physically posting the letter. Worse, it is all too easy to congratulate each other for our online witticisms – indeed, so long as you are funny online, it doesn't seem to matter how cruel you are.

Although the judicial system is slowly catching up with this phenomenon, nevertheless, just like relying on schools, relying on the justice system or on social media gatekeepers to defend your child's honour when someone makes poisonous online statements about your child is giving your power away.

Yes, you should contact the online platform where the bullying is taking place; yes, you should contact the teachers; and yes, you should contact the parents of the online bully. But, no, you shouldn't rely upon these approaches to fix the problem. And really, before all that, the best and quickest way to get this matter resolved is by asking both families to have a polite face-to-face meeting in a bid to ask the offender to remove the post (see Chapter 8).

Anonymous apps

As soon as an anonymous app gets a bad reputation (usually because there are a plethora of suicides associated with it) another anonymous app takes its place and experiences a corresponding rise in popularity. Social media platforms and apps can fall out of popularity quickly, so make sure you keep up to date with what your child is using. At the moment, a lot of teenagers that I know use Whisper and Yik Yak but I have no doubt that these anonymous apps will soon lose their appeal and another anonymous app with some twist or other will take their place.

Whisper is an anonymous social networking app where users post confessions, whether true or false, by superimposing text on a picture. The unique selling point is that Whisper is completely anonymous; users don't have an identity and there are no followers, friends or profiles – the primary way to communicate is to respond to someone else's 'whisper'. The app works by allowing users to add schools or groups and also by using the user's location. In 2014, Whisper was valued at over $200 million.

Going by the slogan 'Yik Yak helps you find your herd', Yik Yak is also a location-based social network that connects users with people nearby. Just to test the waters, even though I am technologically stupid, I found it easy to sign up to Yik Yak with a fake name, fake email address and fake date of birth – and if I can do it anyone can do it. Lots of users spread gossip and rumours on Yik Yak and it can act as a virtual notice board for the local community.

In Dr Michele Borba's book, *UnSelfie: Why Empathetic Kids Succeed in Our All-About-Me World*, it is revealed that there has been a 40% drop in empathy in teens while narcissism has increased by 58%. Borba's book reminds us that we can all be empathy builders and an empathic and compassionate person is less likely to behave badly online.[40]

It's relatively easy to 'block' someone from these sites, but very few teenagers are willing to block people – they want to know what is being said about them and they know that having a high number of followers or friends is socially beneficial. Anyway, unless the service uses heavy defences such as banning an offending user's entire IP address, blocking users is entirely ineffective. A girl I know has about five Facebook pages as she is always getting suspended from Facebook and so she sets up another page with another variation of her name.

It is also easy to use 'parental controls' on some websites, but many of these services are irrelevant – the kids override the parental controls. It is clichéd because it's true – the best way to ensure your child is safe from harm is to maintain open avenues of communication. Most teenagers don't report bullying to their parents because they don't trust how their parents will react – they are afraid the parents will make things worse. They are also afraid that their parents will begin to issue controls over their online life. The most common reason that teenagers give for not telling their parents about online bullying is that they are afraid their parents will restrict their phone usage.

Prevention is better than cure

The fallout from cyberbullying is so extreme that parents need to teach their children how to behave online so that they can see through fake identities, be savvy enough not to post potentially embarrassing pictures and know never to feed the trolls. What is perhaps most destructive about cyberbullying is that shame, horror and humiliation often prevent children from telling anyone – either their parents or their friends. It is for this reason that it is far better to deal with prevention rather than cure when handling cyberbullying.

Check your tech

'Tech savvy and judgement poor' is a dangerous place to be but this is exactly where many teens and tweens are right now. It is only when their judgement has caught up with their tech know-how that they should really be let loose online without supervision. Teenagers have poor impulse control and they take more risks (don't blame your kids for this; this is the fault of biology, so blame Mother Nature) and so, even though they know they shouldn't – just like when we were teenagers and we knew we shouldn't get drunk, smoke or have unprotected sex – kids today often accept friend requests from people they don't know. There are a lot of benefits of having more friends on social media; more likes, more traction and more presence equals more popularity both online and irl.

This is why, every so often, parents and schools need to hold a 'Delete Day' where teenagers get the opportunity to consider their past posts and, as they mature, to delete their more inappropriate online behaviour. Joining an 'I hate the Kardashians' or an 'I hate anyone' Facebook page might have seemed funny at one point in a teenager's life, but six months later they might see that it is a needlessly nasty and dangerous thing to do.

DELETE DAY

The girls at Mary Louis Academy, a Catholic girls' school in Queens, New York, have found that 'Delete Day' works very well for them and they even have a pledge for it.

Delete personal information that is dangerous in public.

Delete unknown 'friends'.

Delete inappropriate comments and pictures.

Delete [anonymous] pages.

Delete hurtful or offensive groups.

Create an email address that is suitable for a college-bound young woman (i.e. not fetishgrrl@hotmail.com).

Encourage my friends to delete!

Inspiring stuff indeed! The beauty of this approach is that not only does it provoke and stimulate discussion and thought among kids, both senior and junior, it also opens up communication about appropriate online behaviour between older and younger teenagers. (See more about Delete Days in Chapter 8.)

Sextortion and scammers

Cyberstalking is becoming ever more prevalent as overseas criminals scour the web for people they can build a rapport with and then deceive them into performing sexual acts on video. These 'catfishers' then use the footage to blackmail their victims for money.

Freckle-faced Ronan Hughes was an immature and guileless 17-year-old from Co. Tyrone when he was the victim of a Romanian-based online criminal gang. Ronan mistakenly believed that he had been interacting with a woman and he was tricked into sending intimate pictures of himself. The gang demanded that Ronan paid them £3,300 or naked pictures of him would be posted to his friends.

Ronan confided in his parents and they went to the police. Sadly, the police didn't help much. According to Ronan's father, Gerard Hughes, 'I knew Ronan was looking for help and I told him [the officer] that all my son wanted is for these images not to be posted. He told us that he couldn't guarantee that. For Ronan, it was totally dismissive. If the police had given Ronan reassurance and said "We'll contact IT experts, we'll close this down, we'll stop that", Ronan would be here today. That's why he came to us [his parents]. He wanted help.'[41]

The couple returned to the police station the next day but they did not hear anything over the next couple of days. This lack of urgency proved fatal.

The axe fell when a friend of Ronan's contacted him to say that she had received a link containing images, but she hadn't opened them. Ronan rang his mother to tell her that the webcam blackmailers had sent his friends the pictures. Ronan's father immediately left work amid concerns about his son but he was too late. Ronan was so overwhelmed by the situation that he took his own life and his father discovered his son's dead body in a field behind their home.

Ronan Hughes' parents spoke out in a courageous and generous bid to help other parents. As Teresa Hughes said, 'We decided to speak out as this is something that could have been prevented. A child with mental illness maybe can't be stopped from taking their own life. But to think that Ronan was living life to the full and then all of a sudden something like this can pop up and take his life … that's why we had to act. We want there to be changes so if a child out there is being bullied online they can go to the police or other authorities with their concerns. We don't want another family to go through what we've gone through.'[42]

Digital sharing

If the worst happens and your teenager has had humiliating pictures posted online by an anonymous poster, it is very important for the parents not to lose their heads. The teenager is already probably feeling vulnerable and ashamed — although they might underplay the situation in a desperate bid to maintain control.

Most parents' first instinct will be to throw the kitchen sink at the situation in a bid to get the pictures deleted. However, if the poster is anonymous, this is usually a complex and quite lengthy process. After the event, you can contact certain agencies and have the offending post removed, but you may not be able to wipe away all traces. Nevertheless, as soon as the crisis strikes, it might be more appropriate to spend the bulk of your time processing the event with your child rather than spending crucial hours distracted by the computer as you try to get the pictures removed. The 48 hours after the crisis strikes are very dangerous.

You can get the pictures removed over the coming weeks, but there have been too many cases of teenagers dying by suicide as soon as the crisis strikes.

On the upside, although it is a sad indictment of society, it isn't necessarily social death to have embarrassing pictures posted. Just like yesterday's papers, it will not necessarily be something that haunts your child for the rest of their lives. Many parents believe that it will ruin their child's future job prospects, but it is unlikely that future employers will search for dirty pictures of prospective employees when they were underage teenagers, and it is wholly inappropriate for an employer to judge prospective employees on their teenage sex life. These pictures are becoming so prevalent that they are not necessarily social ruination.

When I was a teenager, the very worst possible thing to happen was to be judged as a 'slut' in your home town and to become pregnant as a result. Apparently once a girl lost her reputation, it would never be recovered (and no, I didn't live in a Jane Austen novel — this was Dublin in the 1980s and 1990s). When I became an adult I was intrigued when this turned out to be absolute rubbish. Lots of former 'dirty sluts' whose exploits were plastered in graffiti all over my home town went on to become perfectly ordinary women who had perfectly ordinary lives; and no one really cared that they were a 'goer' in their day or that they had a child when they were a teenager.

Similarly, as the years go by, having a sex tape or explicit material emerge from your distant past isn't the social death that many parents presume it to be. It's just sex, after all.

Protective measures

The anonymity available on social media has unleashed a beast, and many weird and grotesque stories of cyberbullying are exposed almost every day. It is fairly easy to make a complaint to Google, Facebook and other search engines and social media platforms, but it can take a long time for a response to be returned. **It is said that the easiest and fastest way to get a page deleted is to make many complaints from different, unique IP addresses.** However, in the meantime, as you're waiting for a response, a lot of damage can be done and so, if your child is being targeted by unknown users, it can be worthwhile paying for a tech expert to bring some damage limitation to the situation.

How to get an image deleted from Google

Google may remove an image if it contains sensitive personal information. 'Sensitive Personal Identifying Information (PII) is defined as information that if lost, compromised, or disclosed could result in substantial harm, embarrassment, inconvenience, or unfairness to an individual.'[43] If the offending image is covered under Google's 'Removal Policies' then the complainant needs to ask Google to remove the image from the search results. If the offending image should be removed for legal reasons then the complainant needs to visit the Google 'Legal Removals' page.

Otherwise, if the image isn't covered under either of these Removal Policies, the complainant needs to contact the site's webmaster to ask them to remove the image. Often this is the best option, although it is the most difficult one. Persistence pays, so continue to request nicely but with powerful reasons why the image should be taken down and it should pay off — learn to be a 'polite nuisance'. Try to ensure that you get in contact with someone who's in charge of managing the particular website and who has the authority to delete the content.

Make sure your email contains the following points:

A brief introduction about who you are and your purpose: 'My name is John Smith and I am the father of Jane. I am emailing you in the hope that you will remove an offensive image of my 14-year-old daughter from your website. As she is under 18 this image is illegal.'

Verify that they are the correct person — 'Are you the correct person to contact about takedown requests?'

Provide a short background about the event — 'She had a boyfriend she trusted, they have now broken up.'

The most important part is the reason why it should be removed — 'This is causing my daughter and my family a huge amount of trauma. We are dreadfully worried about Jane's mental health.'

Ask them to contact you as soon as possible with an answer.

If they have a policy against 'unpublishing', ask them if they would consider blocking the content from being indexed by using robots. txt file or removing her name from the image.

Be gracious and heartfelt. If one person turns you down then ask someone else from the same company. If this doesn't work then the most positive action you can take is to drown the offending post by posting a plethora of positive posts so that a person would have to search very hard to find the negative post.

You can pay agencies to do this for you very effectively. Digital reputation management is a new and growing field — companies are paid to 'game' Google so that negative stories and images can be hidden by swamping the online identity with positive stories and images.

When Sandra's usually affectionate and honest little boy suddenly became moody and secretive, Sandra presumed that teenage hormones were finally kicking in for Brian, her lovable 14-year-old. However, a much darker scenario emerged when one day Brian broke down and told all to his mother.

An older man had infiltrated Brian's online gaming network and he had arranged to meet Brian and his pals in the city later that very day. According to Brian they weren't going to the local disco as planned that night, but instead they were going to this man's apartment to drink alcohol and watch some porn. Brian didn't really want to go but the other boys were really looking forward to it so he was very anxious that Sandra didn't expose him as 'the rat'.

Sandra was in a very precarious position as she didn't want Brian to lose his social standing but she couldn't allow these young boys go to this man's apartment. With some subtle phone calls and fervent promises made among the parents, Sandra managed the situation and the other parents pretended to discover the secret by checking their children's tech.

As the full picture emerged it appeared that the older man had promoted himself as a Steve Jobs-type character with a supposedly impressive head-honcho position in a top tech company. He pretended to be very impressed with the boys' gaming skills and suggested heavily that if they continued to impress him he would be able to get them great jobs in certain tech companies in their future careers. The boys, gullible and impressionable 14-year-olds all, fell for this line and believed their 'gaming skills' were second to none. When the parents went to the police about this man, little could be done as his profile was fake and he had covered his tracks.

The dos and don'ts of dealing with cyberbullying

✓ **Do attend to your child first.** Deal with the content on screen later. Many parents become obsessed with the content and forget that this is the time when the child needs reassurance and love most.

✓ **Do take a screen shot.** Record the evidence if you plan to complain. If you don't, then delete the post immediately.

✓ **Don't feed the trolls.** Teach your kids not to get involved in a back-and-forth with vindictive people — even if they have thought of the perfect retort. Although trolling and vicious social media posts can be very upsetting to anyone, it is worse for teenagers.

✓ **Do ask your child what they worry about online.** Go 'there'. Ask them what they would do if they were attacked online. Explore the different possibilities without discounting any event as improbable. Warn your teenagers that they need never turn to suicide if something awful happens. Everything passes and this too shall pass.

✓ **Do supervise your child's online activity.** A study by the National Anti-Bullying Centre in 2015 found that fewer than 20% of parents supervise their child's online activity. Think of social media as a party that is going on in the next room. Do you know their 'friends'? Predators often have fake profiles and they target teenagers. It only takes one gullible teenager to accept the fake profile as a 'friend' and then they can infiltrate the group as a 'friend of a friend'.

✓ **Do activate parental controls on devices.** Parents should check the 'Restrictions' on tablets and mobile phones as age ratings on downloads and apps can be enforced in the device's settings. Parents can also filter out adult content on Google searches by using Google Safesearch. There are also safety features available from your broadband or phone provider.

✓ **Do teach your kids to watch their online addiction.** Ask them to count how often they check their phone (there's an app called Moment that will do this for you) and if it's too much, see if they can place some limits on it. As a gesture of solidarity, parents can do this with their children as most parents are as bad as their teenagers.

✓ **Do teach your child how to be an upstander online.** Explain to them why they shouldn't press 'like' or 'share' on anything that would cause pain to someone else. They don't have to jump into the middle of a fight, and they needn't commit to any side either. Instead, they can add a calming point or send a sympathetic private message to the target and maybe ask if there is anything they can do to help.

✓ **Do consider how shame might affect your teenager.** Shame is such a destructive emotion that it can pull anyone asunder and prevent them from reacting to a horrible situation. Parents need to discuss with their teenagers how they need not tell them any details but they do need to communicate if they are suffering.

✓ **Don't ban your child from going online.** The chances are that they will disobey this ban and then they will feel painted into a corner if there is further cyberbullying when they shouldn't have been online to see it. Almost every teenager I have counselled about cyberbullying has commented that they would prefer to know what is being said than not know. I couldn't imagine going into a classroom of 30 people knowing that most of them had read horrible comments about me online and I didn't know what they were, and I don't think it's fair to ask any teenager to go through that.

✓ **Do ask your kids to show you their privacy settings.** Ask them how they would report someone or block someone who made them feel uncomfortable or upset. Ask them what information they think is OK to share and what is inappropriate.

✓ **Do keep control of the wi-fi password and social media passwords.** Difficult, I know, but not impossible. Some parents find the 'trust but verify' approach helpful while others prefer to keep their children's online passwords until they have proved themselves emotionally mature enough to handle whatever comes their way. Start out strict and then begin to relinquish control as trust is earned.

✓ **Do discuss public scandals that happen online.** Individuals getting into trouble as a consequence of their online behaviour are often golden teachable opportunities for parents. This is one of the few areas that can engage both teenagers and parents alike and so endless discussions about the rights and wrongs of each case can be very helpful.

✓ **Don't wash your hands of the online world.** This is your child's world and dismissing it simply means that you will have difficulty understanding the subtleties of the situation when a problem arises. If you have absolutely no interest in social media then give a likely teenager a few quid and ask them to teach you the basics of social media every year or so. Having no interest in social media is akin to having no interest in what's going on in teenagers' lives at the local disco or youth club — at best it is foolhardy.

✓ **Do make your kids proud of their social media savvy.** Talk to them about unsafe behaviour and encourage your kids to be proud of their social savvy. Parents take great pains to teach their children how to cross the road safely and not to go off with strangers. Likewise, parents need to talk to their children from a young age about being safe online. This can begin with parents discussing how a photo of themselves that they didn't like was shared all over Facebook and how it was distressing and annoying. It can continue with discussions of other events that happen online that cause upset. Online behaviour should be a common topic of conversation for any engaged family.

How to make a complaint on Facebook

The complainant needs to report the page/post/photo/share in the appropriate category to get it removed. Sometimes the reported content does not get removed as it is not considered to be violating Facebook's terms. If this happens, the complainant should provide feedback explaining why they think it does, and Facebook may reconsider the decision. To report offensive behaviour the complainant needs to go on to the 'Community Standards' page and follow the appropriate link. The Facebook standards show what is and isn't allowed on Facebook. Issues such as threatening behaviour, self-harm, bullying behaviour and exploitation are covered on this page.

Snapchat and your child

It is said that 'delete is the default setting for Snapchat' but this isn't necessarily true as there are many ways to save snaps, chats and stories on this platform. Certainly, most messages from Snapchat automatically expire, but this isn't a reliable way to ensure that it has vanished as image-capture technology such as taking a screenshot is being developed all the time. As with most social media, there are guides for removing content, and parents should take the time to research these. See resources on p. 266.

CyberSafe Ireland

CyberSafe Ireland seek to empower children and parents to 'navigate the online world in a safe and responsible manner'. They run interactive safety sessions with children and they give talks to parents and teachers. The agreement from CyberSafe Ireland on the next page is a clever approach to ensure that children are aware of the inherent dangers involved online.

KIDS

I will protect my personal information online and I won't share my passwords (except with a parent/carer).

I will stop and think before I share photos online.

I will not accept a friend request from anyone I don't know.

I will sit down with my parent/carer and we will work out privacy settings for all my apps and games together.

I will be kind to others and talk to my parent/carer if I'm worried about anything or about what any of my friends are doing online.

I will agree that devices are kept downstairs at night and I will stick to agreed time limits for playing games/being online.

I will allow my parent/carer keep an eye on what I am doing online and I'll talk to them about anything I see, or that I am asked to do, that makes me feel upset or uncomfortable.

PARENTS / CARERS

I will use parental controls (settings that restrict or monitor content/ functionality) as appropriate but I will review these in the future.

I will research safety on new apps that my child wants to use. If I agree that it is okay for them to use an app, we will agree rules and figure out how to apply privacy settings. I will also apply these on my own accounts.

I will think before I share my child's photos online and will ensure that I am only sharing with real-life friends and family.

I will spend time with my child getting familiar with the apps and games that they are using.

I will stay calm, listen and try not to over-react if my child talks to me about something that has happened and I will take advice or appropriate action if I feel that my child or another child is at risk.

_____

By signing this form we agree to all of the above.[44]

8

How to stop bullying
Practical tips

'When I was younger, not being accepted made me enraged, but now, I am not inclined to dismantle my history. If you banish the dragons, you banish the heroes — and we become attached to the heroic strain in our personal history.'

Andrew Solomon

The primary reason anyone has picked this book up is to better understand bullying and to attempt to become part of the solution. Although very widespread, bullying as a serious subject matter perhaps hasn't had as much attention among academics or psychologists as it should have had and until relatively recently, a lot of advice given to targets of bullying has often been unsophisticated and unhelpful. As with all books of this nature, each individual needs to assess all the strategies in this book and take responsibility for the uniqueness of their individual problem by assessing whether each idea would work in their specific set of circumstances. Alcoholics Anonymous have a great saying: 'Take what you need and leave the rest', and this advice could be applied to almost any therapeutic approach. Stopping bullying does not have a one-size-fits-all solution.

Unfortunately, people who are lacking in emotional intelligence can find it difficult to ascertain the merit of any particular advice and they may naively follow unhelpful directions. If your life experience suggests that you often misread other people's motives and behaviour, then you probably need a trusted sounding board to identify what would work and what wouldn't work in your specific situation. Misguided and naive advice can add fuel to the bullies' fire and it is important that the target and the target's family use their critical brain to consider how they should handle their particular problem. If the target innocently and enthusiastically charges into the group of bullies armed only with a speech that has been memorised from a well-meaning parent or self-help book, they can soon find themselves the butt of derision.

All too often teenagers are advised to handle bullying as a mature adult would in the corporate world; by asking the mean kid to meet them in private and to explain that the comments hurt their feelings and that they want it to stop.

Eh, right.

Now, on planet Earth, anyone who has had any dealings with bullying at all will know that the bullies won't meet privately with the target – unless it is to play an elaborate trick on them. More often than not the bullies would laugh in the target's face and relentlessly ridicule them to the rest of the group. They would mercilessly scorn and mimic the target's faux-adult speech and they would immediately see that the target had been advised by an adult. They would then use this episode as a stick to beat them with. Advising the target to do this is just the sort of advice that exacerbates the problem and sets the target up for more ridicule and humiliation.

Other common advice is to 'just ignore them'. However, in mean-kid world, just ignoring the bullies can be incendiary to them and so the bullies push and push in a bid to get a reaction. Of course, when they finally do get a reaction it is generally an emotional outburst and so this is also very dangerous advice.

Parents can also often misread the complexity of the bullying and tell their kids to answer back with one-liners such as, 'you're not so great yourself' or 'you're so immature' or 'we'll see what the principal has to say about that.' But the bullies are often a complex and sophisticated hierarchy of ringleaders, queen bees, sidekicks, wannabes and messengers who are fighting to maintain their status within the group and they will not allow the target to get the upper hand so easily. Mean kids tend to see through a false show of confidence and, just like the reaction to Dodie's attempt at style in Chapter 4, they will immediately reassert their strength so as to punish the target for daring to rise above their station.

Targets are often unused to asserting themselves sufficiently and the bullies intuitively realise this and take advantage of the target's nerves. It's been shown that to stand up to bullies the target needs to assert themselves for eight continuous seconds.[45] But eight seconds is an awfully long time for a previously unassertive child to sustain self-confidence in the face of sneering bullies. The target often blinks first and the bullies then move in for the kill. The majority of teenage targets I have met in the course of my work simply aren't naturally equipped to suddenly act assertively – they can't carry out the advice because they aren't used to being assertive outside their family or friends. When they try to verbally retort their voice goes high-pitched and their body language shows that they don't have the courage of their convictions. This is why telling your child to 'act confident' or 'fight back' is unhelpful and insensitive – it's often not part of their personality to be able to act this way and a parent continuously advising their child to do something they can't do is simply fostering feelings of inadequacy and leading the target to feel self-recrimination and self-loathing. Don't do it.

If your child has already tried to follow your (or someone else's) advice and found that it hasn't worked then the child can become cynical and secretive. The child often then believes that they can't go to their parents for advice because their parents will guide their children towards further humiliation and scorn. Feelings of isolation ensue as they can't confide in their parents any more, for fear of further exacerbating the problem.

Feeling that your problem is insurmountable and there is no one who understands is an incredibly lonely place to be. The target may soon begin to think that nothing will work and that there is nothing for it but to endure the cruelty. The target may also feel conflicting anger and loyalty towards their parents – anger that their parents cannot help them and loyalty that keeps them from telling them exactly how terrible their well-meaning advice turned out to be. This is why concerned adults need to figure out whether the advice they dish out is being carried out correctly and also whether or not their advice is helpful.

When parents are confronted with our children's difficulties, our noble and natural reaction is to do everything in our power to annihilate the difficulty and yet, as the child moves from middle childhood to being a teenager, removing the difficulty is often an inappropriate response. More often connection has more value than solutions – the writer and motivational speaker Brené Brown highlighted this when she said, 'Rarely can a response make something better; what makes something better is a connection.' And so parents are better off ensuring that first and foremost they remember to take the time to authentically connect on a deeper level whenever their teens or tweens come to them with a problem. The days of making everything better are, sadly, over once a child leaves middle childhood and, with this, a new dawn is breaking where deeper relationships matter more than simple solutions.

The following chapter outlines the process whereby parents can lead their children to better relationships – with everyone. This process needs to be examined closely, with a critical eye, as parents and children consider what will work and what might fail in their individual situations – blind devotion to any solution isn't appropriate – instead everyone needs to dig deep and determine how best their loved ones can beat the bullies.

How to handle yourself

The sport of boxing has been shown to have been around for over 3,000 years. Boxing is not only a physical contest but also a battle of wits as boxers need to use their limitations to their advantage while at the same time trying to exploit their opponent's weaknesses. Both the strong and the weak boxer are well aware that one right hook from the stronger boxer will floor the weaker boxer, and yet 'weaker' boxers frequently beat stronger boxers. The reason for this is that any weaker boxer worth their salt will attempt to 'box clever' and outwit their opponent. Likewise, parents of children who have been targeted by bullying need to make sure that their child learns how to box clever.

Parents need to lead the way and show their child that boxing clever is the way to go. However, parents often feel a profound level of rage and helplessness at their position and this can impair their ability to box clever. Parents need a lot of support to help them through this difficult period. Some parents can feel so bewildered by the situation that they can't bear it; they deny the reality of the bullying or they underplay the bullying simply because they can't handle the truth. On the other hand, the red hot rage that can overtake a parent when they first hear about their child being bullied can be harnessed to the child's advantage. But keep the murderous rage and the tears to your own bedroom or your friends' houses or the counselling rooms; to help your child, you will need to ground yourself and ensure that your rage is harnessed so that you can become a strong force to be reckoned with when handling the situation.

Many parents tend to underestimate bullying because the parents can't quite face the fact that their heretofore happy child is being destroyed and so they recoil in horror away from their children's terrible pain. The parents can also underestimate the sophistication of the mean kids' modus operandi – adults are prone to believing that children have pretty basic personalities despite plenty of evidence to the contrary. Parents also often fool themselves (usually because of their own emotional baggage) into believing that their child is more popular than they are and, sometimes, the parents lack the necessary emotional intelligence to understand exactly what is going on in their child's life. If parents are to truly help their child with bullying then they will need to commit to being strictly honest with themselves and be prepared to be more self-aware than might be comfortable.

Most of us don't like to do this because it is too emotional, but if parents can take a moment to close their eyes and cast their mind back to when they were an adolescent in school they might begin to fathom the vast level of complexities that arise in a child's brain every day. When a teenager is in class a whole range of different social and emotional problems are erupting at the same time:

'Will I put my hand up and answer this question? God, everyone will notice me. What if I'm wrong and I look stupid? If I answer right I'll probably just look like a swot, it's probably better to do nothing.' Think about your child and realise that for about seven hours, five days a week they are trying to juggle their actions according to the judgement of perhaps 30 of their peers. Their emotions are in overdrive as they try to figure out what is appropriate and what is not. This is all going on in a nice, easy, boring class under the control of the teacher, so we can multiply these worries by a thousand when it comes to lunch hour.

When should parents step in?

In an ideal world, parents shouldn't be required to step in and fight the child's fights, or at least should stay out of the situation until the children ask for help. Sadly, we don't live in an ideal world, and often parents feel forced to send their children to schools that have a bullying culture and so parents should be ready to step in to help if the child is clearly not coping on their own.

The help that parents provide should mostly centre on providing considered advice, emotional support and physical protection to their own child without needing to directly fight the perpetrator. This doesn't mean that a gentle and passive child should be required to change in any way — more that targets of bullying need to accept who they are and develop the aspects of their personality that can save them from being bullied. For example, maybe the child is a good and loyal friend, or maybe they are funny so they can make people laugh at an opportune moment, or maybe they are sensitive and so can spot a troubling situation before others can. Parents might also remind their children just how ineffective strategies such as hiding from the bully are as they didn't work previously and probably won't work in the future.

When parents do decide to step in and take action, this is a crucial moment in the arc of the bullying experience. The intervention needs to be effective, because if it fails, the child will feel all security fading away. And so the parent will need to gather up their strength and dig deep for this.

It is important for everyone — parents and children — to learn from each experience and keep in mind each success and failure. In the future, parents can then remind their child how they faced down the bully in the schoolyard by using their wit, by using distraction, by spotting the potential upstander or by assertively and continuously requesting help and support.

Parents also need to admit when their advice and support did not work. Many parents self-assuredly insist that their child mustn't have followed their advice correctly because otherwise it would have worked, but the parents might not know all the story — the child may have chosen to tell only one part of it for some reason or another. Parents need to be sensitive to this and realise that sometimes their advice isn't appropriate for the child and so the family might need to regroup and take stock.

As our children move from babies to toddlers through middle childhood and the teen years, so we parents move from being physical caretakers of our children to providing a role of mentoring and guidance. And so, although we can help, support, guide and encourage our children, by the time our children have become teenagers it is often neither appropriate nor helpful for the parent to try to solve the teenager's problems. Madeleine Levine, in her powerful book *The Price of Privilege*, describes how parents need to allow their children to go through a certain level of emotional pain if they are to grow and develop: 'By allowing [kids] to get occasionally bruised in childhood we are helping to make certain that they don't get broken in adolescence. And by allowing them their failures in adolescence, we are helping to lay groundwork for success in adulthood.' The teenager needs to learn how to handle bullies. If the parent steps in and mows everyone down then there will inevitably be further bullying incidents in the future. Although it is appropriate for children under the age of 12 to assume the adults will sort it all out, on some level, teenagers will need to refrain from automatically assuming that the nearest adult will rescue them – when a child enters the teen years they should be starting to learn how to handle themselves.

As Eleanor Roosevelt wisely advised, 'To handle yourself, use your head; to handle others, use your heart,' so it can be beneficial if teenagers learn something about the apparent weakness that triggered the bullies to attack. This might be a weakness in society, a weakness in the school environment, a weakness in the bullies or a weakness in the target. Knowledge is power and the child will be better equipped if they learn something about the situation rather than acting as if the difficult behaviour landed from Pluto and the only thing a person can do is to look to the authorities or their parents to take the 'evil' away.

Teenagers need to learn how to think for themselves so that one day if they are involved in a complicated peer group situation, they can figure out the best route to take. No matter how much we wrap our kids in cotton wool, at some point, whether it is when they are 14, 16 or 18 years old, they will probably be offered some drugs, or offered a lift from a drunk but cool friend, or engaged inappropriately online – and your teenager will have to make a decision on their own. If teenagers are to learn how to handle themselves, they will need to have some practice in learning to rely on themselves. The parent can come up with helpful ideas and different options but the teenager will probably need to be the one who has to try them out. The parents can open the door but the teenager must walk through.

Preparing your children about possible future events that are bound to happen enables them to be prepared for the curveballs that life often throws us. The acclaimed writer Andrew Solomon gives an inspiring TED talk about 'How the worst moments in our lives make us who we are' and in this talk Solomon advises that 'Oppression breeds the power to oppose it.'[46] If the parent can impart the idea that problems can cause difficulties but they are rarely insurmountable then the parent has set the tone for the children to feel capable and able for the challenges they will face in life. Unless you think your child is in actual danger, sometimes you need to trust that your child can handle the situation and the best you can offer them is to hope for the best, prepare for the worst and cheer them on from the sidelines.

How to open a dialogue with your child

The first thing a parent needs to do when confronted with a bullying situation is to gather as much information as possible. The parent needs to chat subtly, sensitively and comprehensively with their child, with their children's friends, with their children's friends' parents and with relevant teachers so as to ascertain the whole picture. It can also be helpful to chat with an aunt or someone who has known your child for a long time so that they can add an objective perspective.

Dismissing the bullies as 'pure evil' is rarely helpful, nor is deciding that it is a simple case of racism or homophobia or jealousy, etc. Although such clear comments often make everyone feel a fleeting sense of satisfaction, it is usually too simplistic an analysis of what is taking place. It is much more helpful to attempt to understand the complexities behind the attack. While intolerance, racism or homophobia might be at the root of the problem, there are usually other issues that also need to be addressed, such as the school environment, the bully's personality, the bystander effect and a culture of bullying.

Sometimes, because of privacy matters, it won't be possible to get everyone's version, but it is imperative that the parent and child discuss in intimate detail the incidents that happened and it is vital that the parents approach these conversations with an open, non-judgemental ear. Although the detail of the incidents is important, if your child doesn't want to reveal the actual name they are being called ('easy-spread', 'little dick', 'Shay has herpes', etc.) there is no major need for this to be pressed out of them. Everything else is more important than the actual name.

Many parents immediately fly off the handle when they hear the cruelties that their child has been exposed to. However, parents need to be better than that if they are to achieve a productive result. Parents need to keep their rage and emotions in check as they encourage their child to open up. The following questions might help parents stay focused:

- When did it first happen?

- Why did it first happen?

- What happened after the first incident?

- Why did the bullying/teasing/hostility/behaviour continue after the first incident?

- How did it continue?

- What is unhelpful? What makes it worse?

- What is helpful? What makes it better?

- Who are the bystanders?

- Who are the sympathetic bystanders?

- Who, of the bystanders, might be brave enough to help?

- What is preventing the bystanders from being upstanders?

- What is the position of the authorities (the teachers)?

- Is there any teacher who might be more helpful than others?

This will help you open your eyes to the bigger story as well as ensuring that you can better empathise with your child. Although your child may believe that they are being bullied, the actual bullying might not be as severe as you fear. Your child might be unused to conflict or maybe hasn't learned the appropriate social skills in certain social situations and is receiving negative reinforcement from their peers as a consequence. Although this isn't bullying, it still feels bad for the child and so the parent should still try to improve the situation. Perhaps you could offer your child some new options that haven't been previously considered. The real question in a situation such as this is: 'What is helpful and what is unhelpful?'

As the child moves from middle childhood to their teenage years the communication between child and parent can become closed down. This distancing is a natural and necessary aspect of maturity, although parents can often feel hurt and offended by the closed door from their hitherto open and straightforward little girl or boy. It is a fine line between ensuring that the lines of communication remain open while at the same time permitting the child to have a private life – but this is the balance that the parents have to try to strike.

If the parent suspects bullying is taking place the avenue of communication needs to be opened as a matter of urgency. This might be done by creating a regular, weekly event that allows unfettered conversation to take place. Maybe you could give them a lift somewhere regularly (and insist on no screens as a return for the favour) or you could go out for lunch or a milkshake in their favourite restaurant (again, no screens!). This needs to be an opportunity for the parent and child to meet one-on-one, so having other children around during this special time is inappropriate. For many families it will be difficult to create this space but the importance of it cannot be underestimated. Sometimes it can be effective if the parent sets the tone by confiding some age-appropriate things to their child – perhaps there were some snide comments made in the office where you work and you felt that you should have spoken up and been an upstander but instead you took a lower road and stayed schtum. Admitting your weaknesses can be the royal road to recovery as your child begins to realise that no one is perfect and it is OK not to be OK.

The majority of your children's social interactions will take place at school or online and so it is imperative that the parent is sensitive to both the school environment and their online life.

If your child is being bullied online then the online environment needs to be analysed just as thoroughly as the schoolyard. This will mean that your child needs to open up about their online activities so that you can help them explore the dynamics. This isn't the time to begin preaching at your teenagers about disobeying you – instead, this is a crucial time to reconnect with your child by standing shoulder-to-shoulder with them in their hour of need. If you have no idea of your child's social media activity, now is the time to change that. Ask your child to allow you some access to their social media presence; although it might not be appropriate to have full access, it is also inappropriate to have no access – the parent holds the keys to the kingdom as it is they who are usually paying for the wi-fi. (See the agreement on p.189.)

If your child's school is an environment that dismisses bullying, then your approach will need to be very different from an environment where such incidents are taken very seriously. Many children, especially those in their early teens, judge themselves on their ability to be popular among their peers. Being popular at this age is generally shaped by the child's ability to fulfil the gender roles; i.e. the popular boys are athletic, handsome and confident, and the top girls are pretty and social. If your child doesn't fit into these particular boxes then ostracism or exclusion is more likely and the parent needs to be sensitive to these prevailing winds.

Of course, many will argue that this is morally wrong. You may want to fight this mentality, but perhaps you can do this on your own time and in the meantime help your child in the middle of their crisis. Leading your child into a life of social martyrdom is not a helpful path. Even if the parent chooses to fight against social injustices, they often need to accept that their child has fallen victim to these social mores. Arguing with your child about why they shouldn't care about the opinions of the bullies might be an interesting moral point but it can add to your child's emotional trauma as the bullying continues and the parents are distracted by their moral crusade.

If the school environment is competitive, insecure and aggressive, it is likely that bullying will take place. Changing the bullying atmosphere will take parents some time and so, in the meantime, parents should make a strong bid to target certain classes or areas within the school. For example, perhaps your child is often excluded at lunchtime – and so perhaps you can be the parent who insists that certain initiatives are brought into the school at lunchtime?

How to communicate with the school

Many parents avoid communicating with the school in the misguided belief that no news is good news and because they don't want to look like troublemakers. However, it seems astonishing that we expect the school to understand the intricacies of our children's peer relationships and yet we seldom communicate with them to help teachers better understand these nuances.

It is important that parents begin an easy communication right from the start with teachers so that if a problem arises everyone is already familiar with each other. Parents can volunteer their time in the school so that they get to know the school culture from the inside out; they can offer to fund-raise for certain provisions that would make the school a better place or they can arrange a short meeting with certain teachers to pre-empt any concerns that the parent would like the teacher to know about.

Viewing the teachers as the distant enemy is unhelpful and parents need to grasp the nettle and informally make themselves known to the teachers. In very large schools it can be impossible for the teachers to get to know every parent; however, with some astute judgement, the parent can quickly figure out which teacher or year head they need to become acquainted with.

Sometimes it is the teacher or even the principal who is the bully. This tricky situation needs to be handled with shrewd intelligence – just because the 'authorities' have the power doesn't mean that you, the parent, or your child doesn't have any power in this situation. The child is well advised to learn to keep their distance from bullying teachers – in all walks of life we will meet difficult people that circumstances force us to get along with – and this might be the learning curve for your child to learn how to handle difficult people. However, if the situation is unbearably toxic an onslaught of continuous written complaints from the parents and an insistence on meetings after every incident should ensure that the bully in authority learns to refrain from picking on your child – because they know there will be a series of strongly-worded complaints and meetings about it if they don't.

Most second-level schoolteachers aren't bullies, and mostly they are focused upon looming exams; they want to help with the social and behavioural issues but they often believe that the academic issues take precedence over the social concerns. Whether this is right or wrong is irrelevant; what matters is that the parent of a child who is being bullied needs to realise how much and how often schools tend to be distracted by academic issues and so end up underplaying accusations of bullying. (Think about when you are under severe pressure in work and someone comes in with a complaint from left field – often our immediate reaction is to dismiss it, pass the buck and underplay it because we feel that it just isn't our role to deal with it.)

Principals and teachers are as human as the rest of us and wild finger-pointing merely leads the school authorities to believe that your entire family are hysterical. The parents need to show instead that they are serious people who will not be easily dismissed.

If the parents wish to nip a nasty trend in the bud then this is exactly what they should say: 'We wish to nip in the bud a nasty tendency that is growing in this classroom.' Don't mention the

B-word unless you are sure it can be described as bullying – parents can still request immediate action to ensure that nasty behaviour is dealt with without alleging that bullying is taking place.

When a child is new to the school, teething problems need to be consistently monitored so that little problems don't become bigger. Different strategies can be tried – such as identifying likely upstanders, learning to read what it is that ignites the bullies further, becoming more self-aware of the consequences of their own behaviour and figuring out how to become a more difficult person to bully – but the parents need to check in each time to see if the strategies have worked. If the parents have advised the child to 'ignore the teasing but respond strongly to any taunting and speak privately to a certain teacher if taunting occurs' then, in theory, the child will be ready and will know what to do if the teasing turns to taunting. The parent should have already helped them to pre-identify the teacher they will speak to and the parent perhaps should speak to this teacher privately to warn them that this issue is unfolding.

Initially, the parent might approach the class tutor and explain the situation. If there is little or no improvement in the situation then the parent will need to escalate their complaint and request an appointment with the class tutor, the year tutor and the school counsellor – or whoever seems appropriate. The point of this meeting is to show that you are a force to be reckoned with and you will not be dismissed easily. At this meeting, the parents can insist that some specific anti-bullying speakers or initiatives be brought into the school as soon as possible as well as some direct and appropriate sanctions for the aggressor.

At the meeting with the teacher the parents can ask them these direct questions:

- What measures will you take to ensure that my child doesn't feel threatened when they are in school?

- When will these measures be taken?

- How will I know when these measures have been taken?

By asking these questions the parent is putting the onus on the school to come up with a definite plan and to communicate with you when they have put the plan in action. Parents need to be articulate and strong as many schools tend to underplay the situation and wave away the concerned parents with calm and bland reassurances. Parents need to be prepared for this response and they should have with them a copy of the school's anti-bullying policy – usually easily found online – already highlighted and be prepared to quote relevant aspects of it.

In the meantime, the parent should be working with their child to analyse the situation in depth so that the child begins to figure out which approach works better than others. *The child will need to be as involved in the solution as the parents and the school* – this is a complex process that needs a lot of effort from everyone. If the child is falsely reassured that the parents will take care of it then they will feel doubly hurt when this turns out not to be true. There may be lots of false dawns while your child tries to desperately convince you (and themselves) that the bullying has gone away but it is unlikely to simply vanish into thin air. Although parents need to be prepared to give the strategies some time to work, nevertheless speed is of the essence as every day that goes by is causing emotional harm to your child. Not only that, but unfortunately, although the bullying may die down when you and your child are working together to combat it, it can often rear its head when the eye is taken off the ball. Parents need to be ready to re-address the problem every time it comes back – as the old Japanese proverb tells us, 'Fall seven times and stand up eight.'

How to introduce school initiatives

Sadly, many of the parents of bullied children I meet in my office often feel hamstrung and paralysed by the dismissive attitude of the school. This is where the parent will need to dig deep and brave the sarcastic remarks that will be directed towards them. They may need to operate outside their comfort zone for some months as they insist on certain initiatives taking place. It won't be easy, but parents need also to ensure that the school provides children with the opportunity to speak out about nasty and bullying behaviour without feeling the world will end if they make a noise. Parents can also insist that anti-bullying iniatives are put in place with a calm and controlled response, ensuring that the whole place doesn't blow up once 'bullying' is mentioned, with everyone losing their head and pointing the finger at everyone else.

It is a rare school that isn't prepared to work with the parents on some level to minimise bullying. If a concerned parent wishes to reduce bullying and power plays in a school, the easiest and most effective way to do this is to promote kindness. It could be argued that Henry James unlocked the key to the secrets of the universe when he advised, 'Three things in human life are important. The first is to be kind. The second is to be kind. And the third is to be kind.' If the school environment can promote kindness, there will be less need to focus on all the dastardly aspects of human nature. Most humans like to feel kind; we like the feeling of benevolence it bestows upon us and studies show that if we do a good deed we are more likely to look for another good deed to do so as to confirm our sneaking suspicion that we are only great.

If a teacher can set a tone of kindness and forbearance in a class then, like ripples across the ocean, the children in this classroom will be positively infected by the kindness. Below are some specific suggestions you can suggest to your schools to help foster this tone of kindness and friendliness among tweens and young teenagers.

✓ **Sociogram.** The class teacher constructs a sociogram by asking a series of questions probing for affiliations between classmates. Although a certain level of sensitivity is required for this process, the diagram can then be used to identify pathways for friendship between warring factions.

✓ **Buddy Bench.** This can be very effective in promoting a culture of kindness and understanding. A certain bench is painted by the children in a group. Whenever a child has no one to play with, they can sit on the bench. It is up to the school to ensure that the Buddy Bench is operated appropriately and kindly.

Buddy Bench Ireland

I spoke to Sam Synnott from Buddy Bench Ireland and she explained how the organisation works. Sam pointed out that, more than anything, the Buddy Bench gives children the required tools to build their emotional intelligence — the actual bench is, in many ways, a symbol of kindness. Buddy Bench Ireland come into the school with a workshop that includes roleplays and exercises. At a reasonably low cost, this can be very effective as a way to create a positive atmosphere in a school that is marred by drama. Buddy Bench Ireland divide their workshops into different age groups:

Little Buddies (up to about age 7): These kids totally embrace the Buddy Bench and through this they learn empathy and responsibility and the concept of being an upstander.

Buddy Bench Juniors (ages 7–9): For this age group, the Buddy Bench programme goes a bit deeper and explains to the kids how to deal with their emotions in a positive manner and how sometimes your body might be sending you emotional signals — such as your tummy feeling queasy when you're feeling nervous. These kids are sitting on the cusp of the tween and teen years; they love the idea of being kind and looking after the younger kids but they are getting a little bit too cool to use it for their peers.

Buddy Bench Seniors (ages 9–12): Workshops are run for this age group to foster a culture of kindness; the Buddy Bench is merely used as a visual tool to remind the kids of the motto 'Look up, look around and look out for each other.' Mindfulness, mind-maps and other strategies are used to promote self-awareness. The 'Be a Hero' programme is especially effective for this age group to empower the child with a feel-good factor that creates a culture of kindness.

✓ **Emotional intelligence workshops.** These should be pre-identified by the parent before they are proposed — with obstacles such as the costs involved anticipated and appropriate speakers identified beforehand. An effective speaker coming in to give a series of talks can have a very significant impact on a group of children. The parents' association can come up with the titles of the talks so that they can be directed at certain troubling issues, such as 'Bullying and Difficult Friendships' or 'The Importance of Kindness' or 'Cyber-Safety'.

✓ **Worry box.** The worry box should be placed in every classroom and the children should be invited every so often to write their worries and post them into the box. The worries can be anonymous or not — the point of the exercise is that the school establishment has the opportunity to nip any troubling situations in the bud. Of course, these boxes can be used cynically, but they can also alert teachers to the general atmosphere in the school, whether children feel threatened and what darker forces are shaping the school environment.

✓ **Anti-bullying ambassadors.** Anti-bullying ambassadors can be picked from each class to serve as people who are expected to keep company with younger kids who seem lost or lonely. The anti-bullying ambassadors can take it in turns to chat with certain children so that one child isn't always left to handle the same child. These ambassadors can be changed (or not) as the months go by so as to ensure any power plays get nipped in the bud. Anti-bullying ambassadors can be encouraged to gently confront peers on bullying behaviour. The offences — such as isolating other kids, being mean, hurting someone's feelings and taunting — can be devised by the children and written on anti-bullying posters for the school walls.

Anti-bullying ambassadors

If required, the anti-bullying ambassador initiative can be established on a formal basis. The Diana Award's Anti-Bullying Campaign spearheads such an initiative. Personalised training days can be delivered within the school setting for 30 students, equipping the students with the knowledge and skills they need to tackle bullying and raise awareness of issues such as isolation, taunting and teen drama. Bespoke packages for each school can be provided with assemblies, workshops and talks with parents to ensure that change can take place within the school environment. Every anti-bullying ambassador receives some accoutrements for their role and also a certificate and guide for parents. See antibullyingpro.com.

✓ **Random acts of kindness.** Children can be encouraged to perform random acts of kindness. This cultivates a culture of kindness within the school that can create more ripples than many parents expect. Kind acts should be rewarded and acknowledged within the school. Larger initiatives such as charitable initiatives or visits to homeless projects can promote feelings of charity and generosity; however, smaller, more intimate gestures such as inviting a child to have lunch at their table should also be taken seriously and appreciated. If you, as a parent, are feeling flush, you could donate a few prizes to set the ball in motion. Yes, it will cost you, yes, that will be annoying, but it may begin something special — so it could be worth it.

✓ **Restorative justice.** Restorative justice is becoming more and more widely used as a means to combat anti-social behaviour in society. Some see this as an optimistic view of human nature but others argue that it is more realistic; it is better to teach people how to behave better than to merely punish them. Restorative justice works as it doesn't allow the aggressor to turn off their moral engagement so easily and because it isn't particularly punitive. The target is required to identify the damage that has been done and the offender is required to repair the harm they've done. This process is rarely simple or easy and it needs to be handled with sensitivity and care by the teacher. The bully can often be in deep pain and the target can find it very difficult to trust this process. However, if it is done well, it can be very powerful for everyone concerned.

✓ **Meditation and mindfulness.** Meditation and mindfulness programmes can be very effective in reducing mindless aggression and tension within the classroom.

✓ **Online safety workshops.** There are many different organisations (such as CyberSafe Ireland) and speakers who can be booked to run workshops promoting online safety among children, and also workshops that help teachers and parents navigate the cyber world.

✓ **Seasonal one-to-one meetings with the head tutor or school counsellor.** This can be effective as a way to nip troubling situations in the bud.

✓ **Peer mediation.** If done correctly and properly structured, mediation can be a powerful problem-solving strategy for schools

✓ **Delete Day.** Get the computer class involved in good online etiquette. Hold a 'Delete Day' with senior students guiding junior students so that they can explore online behaviour and ask questions that they would be reluctant to explore with adults. If this is held in public in school and run mostly by senior students, it also gives younger teenagers (who most often become involved with the latest anonymous site or app that has hijacked the school) the opportunity to chat with older, cooler kids about their experiences and how these sites can lead to disturbing behaviour.

Anti-bullying programmes

There have been many recent studies on the effectiveness of anti-bullying programmes in schools and it turns out that the programme needs to be interesting if it is to be effective and many students find these programmes boring and repetitive.[47] Bland and negative messages such as 'Don't be a bully' and 'Bullying is nasty' get tuned out and programmes that are a good deal more engaging and inspiring than that are required.

Often, when a bully is identified, the only real punishment he or she will receive is suspension, or, in really drastic cases, expulsion (which rarely actually happens) and many targets fear retaliation for 'snitching' more than anything else. This is why the resolution to bullying needs to be multi-pronged and comprehensive — punishing the bully just isn't effective enough. If the students get a sense that the adults in charge won't be able to stop the bullying when the bully returns to school, then they understandably shy away from leaving themselves exposed and vulnerable. Anonymous reporting is an essential tool that needs to be introduced into every school so as to protect the targets from retaliation.

The effectiveness of such programmes usually depends largely upon the school's commitment to their anti-bullying guidelines. Bullying is often racist, homophobic and/or sexist and so programmes that focus upon tolerance for difference, kindness, empathy and awareness can be more effective than straightforward 'anti-bullying' programmes. Effective anti-bullying measures target the entire school and not a specific problem class. Workshops that teach emotional wellbeing, assertiveness skills, coping mechanisms, social skills and anger management can also be very successful at creating a culture of acceptance and tolerance and an upstanding mentality. Likewise, classroom-based teaching, seasonal initiatives and other school-based campaigns can be fruitful, especially if they are engaging and inspiring.

Thankfully, we have an increasingly more progressive education system and 'well-being' is now being taught as a subject in the Junior Cycle in Irish schools. As a direct result of this, we will now have many more teachers who are qualified to teach programmes in the area of mental health.

How to handle the unhelpful school

When an aeroplane hits turbulence, parents are advised to put their oxygen masks on first. By the same token, parents should always ensure that they are emotionally prepared to face the emotional horror involved with dealing with a bullying situation. It is very important that the parents obtain extra support at this emotionally fraught time either through professional counselling or some other structured support. The very essence of your family is being attacked and if you pretend to yourself that you can handle this then you are in danger of being less helpful to your children as a consequence of your pride and your emotions.

As has been mentioned, some schools minimise and dismiss the bullying in a lazy bid to pretend to themselves that they are running a tight ship. The teacher and the school principal might be very kind and sympathetic to the parents of the target but they can still be completely ineffective in dealing with the bullies in the school. It is imperative that the parent becomes sensitive to the school environment and records everything that takes place. For example, if you feel you are being subtly undermined when you complain it is important that you articulate this in your notes. Tedious, I know, but when we consider what the child is going through, and what you as a parent are up against, it's the very least we can do.

Every meeting with the school should be followed up by a letter. If writing isn't your strong point you might look for someone who can help you with this, or else you could show your inner strength by owning it – mention in the letter that writing isn't your forte but this doesn't make your points any less valid; it just means a little more time and effort might be needed to make yourself clear.

As bullying can be subtle – often made up of comments, looks, 'accidental' nudges and exclusion – it is all too easy for the school to underplay it. Not only that, but bullies can be interpersonally cleverer than the target; they can stick together and lie so that it looks as though the target has made things up or misunderstood the situation. This makes it easier for the teacher to underplay the situation but again, with a letter that identifies and highlights the modus operandi of the bullies, then the parent is armed to request a comprehensive response.

The involved parents do have some power but they need to use it appropriately if they are to be effective. They need to ask for the child's records – parents are entitled to see them – and they need to learn how to be a 'polite nuisance' until the matter is resolved. Parents should become very closely acquainted with the school's complaint procedure and its bullying policy, and they need to stay away from oral discussions that aren't achieving very much and instead opt for letters, records and formal meetings. The reason for this is that although oral discussions can be personally satisfying in the short term, in the long term they can be ineffective. Formally arranged meetings are often more effective than a quick word before or after class. The following is a sample letter that a parent could send to the principal or the year head if they don't feel there has been an adequate response from the teacher.

Dear _____

I enclose copies of correspondence with the year head of first year, Miss Lynch, describing how my daughter Laura continues to be bullied by Allie Green and her friends. Can you please inform me what measures the school intends to introduce to deal with the ongoing bullying? The response so far has been unsatisfactory because [the bullying has not stopped/I have not been told what the school is doing about the problem].

I am requesting a formal investigation into my complaint and I need to be kept informed on a [daily/weekly/monthly] basis about the measures taken to ensure my child doesn't feel threatened in school. I note from Laura's records that [bullying incidents have been recorded/bullying incidents have not been recorded] and [the file fails to reveal what action was taken/the file reveals action was taken but it has not been successful]. Can you please tell me how you have dealt with other complaints of bullying within the school so that I can know what type of strategies to expect?

As per your anti-bullying policy and complaints procedure that I have read and reviewed [quote here] can you please communicate with me the help and support that Laura will receive from the school staff to ensure her safety at this school? Also, will you please send me the exact procedure you aim to follow in order to resolve this issue? As this situation is causing significant emotional harm to my child, I need a detailed reply to this letter within five working days.

Yours truly,

_____

Of course, many schools are exceptionally efficient at waving away parents' concerns and informing the parents that the 'case is closed' whenever the school deems it to be. However, no matter what the principal says, the case isn't closed if you are unhappy with the situation, and if you are unhappy with the so-called solution, then you need to calmly and clearly state that, from your perspective, the case isn't closed at all. Indeed, this might be the time to point out to the principal that you will be forced to take the matter up with others if you don't get adequate resolution; the board of management, the department of education and the police are other parties that can be addressed if the principal isn't adequately engaged in resolving the situation.

On the other hand, it is important that highly emotional Mama Bears don't lose their heads and mindlessly blame the school for the outrageous behaviour of a bully. This is the time for the parent to be serious, to be forceful, but most of all, to be effective – losing your temper is for less important events; for something as serious as bullying you need to have your wits about you.

Many parents agonise over whether they should allow their children to change schools and, of course, they're right to agonise: it's a big decision and not one to be made lightly – and the big risk is that the bullying might continue in the new school. So should you stand and fight or should you leave for higher ground?

If you strongly agree with the following then perhaps the best thing you could do for your child is to move schools.

✓ The current school has the traits of the classic bullying environment

✓ The authorities are ineffective in handling bullying.

✓ Your child has a disposition that will make them a target of further bullying.

✓ The bullying has gone on for so long that it would be impossible for the child to assimilate back into the schoolchildren's social world.

If you are moving schools because of bullying then you need to clearly tell the new school about your child's previous experiences. Fully describe your child's disposition to them and ask for their help in transitioning your child to the new school. In the meantime, it would help your child if you could reactivate some old friendships or identify some pleasant pursuits your child could follow as they are transitioning into the new school – they'll need all the back-up they can get at this difficult time.

When changing schools, you will need to examine the new school with a critical eye. Some people are of the view that a smaller school means that there is less bullying, but in my experience the size of the school doesn't matter – it's the school environment and the attitude of the school authorities to the bullying that holds the most weight.

The environment matters more to some children than others. Some children really need a nurturing environment while for others it doesn't matter so much. Not only that, some children need a lot of support as they enter a new environment while others will just rock on in. Parents need to accept and be attuned to the child they have and ascertain what support they can give their children at these periods of transition.

Before parents decide to move, they should ask the prospective school about their approach to bullying. Explain that it is for this reason that you are moving and ask them what supports they will provide for your child to ensure they settle in. If you are taken seriously when you say this, it's a good sign. If there are regular anti-bullying talks, initiatives and workshops (from visiting professionals in the field, not from the teachers), for both parents and students, this also suggests that the school takes bullying seriously. If, on the other hand, the school is proud to point to their anti-bullying policy, their anti-bullying posters and the anti-bullying week that the teachers run during term time, this suggests that the school's attitude to bullying is a bit sluggish and could do with more progressive thinking. Have a look at local online forums to figure out the new school's strengths and weaknesses, and don't be afraid to ask questions – indeed, you might have to be a 'polite nuisance' at this point as well. Some schools are very 'cliquey', while other schools are very friendly and welcoming.

Sometimes it is advisable for the child to be moved quickly – before any lasting damage has occurred – but in other situations the damage has been done and so the parents might then take their time to ensure their child is helped to choose the right new school. Many parents choose not to move their child if the child only has a few months left in the school year, but most parents and children that I have worked with have bitterly regretted this decision as it has caused profound damage in between times.

How to handle the bully's parents

This is a very tricky issue and handling the bully's parents depends on the parents in question. If the parents are difficult then there is little point in hoping that they'll suddenly exclaim, 'You're right! My child is a bully and I'd better put a stop to it!' If the bully's parents are bullies themselves then it is more helpful if you leave them to it and go elsewhere looking for resolution – to the school authorities, to the concerned bystanders and to your child's own strengths. In the course of my work I have been confronted with many appalling situations where the bully is blindly supported by the parents. There is little point in going to the well when the well is dry and neither is it useful to put yourself in a situation where the bully's parents might insult you or your children, so a certain level of self-protectiveness might be necessary in some cases. If, however, they seem reasonably decent individuals, then it is very much in your interests to put your best foot forward in an attempt to bring about some reconciliation between the children.

The most important element of handling this situation is to consider what it is you need from the offender's parents. The parents of children who are being accused of bullying behaviour are instinctively incredibly defensive – no matter how friendly or reasonable the accuser is – and so a request for a very specific resolution will be more easily handled than general comments about bullying behaviour. If, in order to prevent more damage being caused to your child, you need the parents' support and you need their co-operation, then you need to keep this to the forefront of your mind in every meeting. The defensive anger of the offender's parents cannot be underestimated. They are often determined to prove that it was just high jinks on the part of their child, or their child was driven to it by your child's behaviour, or someone else is to blame, or blah, blah, blah. It is seldom very helpful to drive your whole point home at this stage – instead, keep to the task in hand; if you want the page taken down you keep repeating this request. It's not your job to teach these parents how to parent their child – choose your battles wisely. The point that their child is a vindictive little brat can be kept for another conversation. It will be very hard for parents not to get side-tracked by the general nastiness of the behaviour and discussing exactly who is to blame, but it will rarely be helpful. The most helpful strategy is to continuously repeat your very specific request, calmly and with total focus.

It can become very difficult when the parents are friendly with one another and one child turns on the other child. At this point the parents need to consider whether their friendship is important and should be separated from the fight or whether the friendship between the parents was merely a relationship of convenience that was borne out of regular meetings. Self-awareness is crucial at this point so that parents don't become overwrought with expectancy from their 'friends'.

This is a meeting that needs to go well. There is absolutely no point in meeting the bully's family if you are going to spew your anger; vent your rage somewhere else and keep your cool for this meeting. For an incident that has happened online, a conciliatory and focused face-to-face meeting that requests the offender to take the post down is more effective than a meandering and emotional meeting that directs anger at the offender. If one of the parents can't contain themselves, then they shouldn't attend the meeting. If neither parent can, then perhaps they should ask a friend, a relative or a counsellor to make the request on their behalf.

You need to identify exactly what is your desired outcome – do you want the offending behaviour stopped or perhaps it is an online post or page that needs to be deleted? Do you want the bully to ignore your child for ever more? Or do you think that the kids can be pulled back from the brink and become friends again? You should have a Plan A and Plan B identified in your mind before the meeting.

The victim's parents set the tone and whichever parent is more self-controlled, calm and conciliatory is the parent who should make contact, requesting a meeting at the other family's convenience. If a calming voice such as a counsellor or mediator is necessary as both parents of the target are very distressed, then the parents can explain that they are asking the mediator to be present to ensure that everyone stays civil.

If they agree to your specific request then you need to ask exactly when they will do it and, most important, how your child will know that things have changed. Will the aggressor smile at the target from now on or would you prefer if they ignored each other? Or perhaps you can request that the bully refrains from speaking to or about your child? Be clear about what your child needs. Perhaps the parents can ask the bully to remove an offensive online post on the spot. If not, it can be helpful for parents to request that they are messaged once the post/page has been taken down.

If necessary, arrange a meeting for the following week (or even the following day if the issue is urgent) to check in with progress – this can be done on the phone but it might not be appropriate. You might request that this second meeting is only held if the behaviour is still a problem, e.g. the post/page isn't removed, and perhaps it should take place in the school or the police station. Most civilised countries have laws about 'hate speech' and it is for this reason that you can request a meeting in these locations. In Ireland, complaints are often made with the support of the Irish Council of Civil Liberties and the 1989 Incitement to Hatred Act is the law that protects citizens from such nasty behaviour. Of course, it is a crime to possess, take, make, distribute or show indecent images of a person under 18 years of age.[48]

If the offender's family are having difficulty taking down or deleting the post/page then it is imperative that the target's family helps with the tech know-how. It is for this reason that the target's parents should have properly researched before the meeting exactly how to delete the post/page in question so there can be no doubt about the situation. The target's family should go online before any meeting and find a computer expert who is willing to help with any tech problems. You can pay an IT specialist for this service and it can be done remotely so long as the offender gives the password to the tech expert. Yes, it might be very frustrating for the target's family to shell out cash for this; however, in view of the damage being caused to your child, it is worth it.

This is not the time to clear up the entire situation – a process of restorative justice within the school system may one day do that, but this will take a long period of time. Speed is of the essence if an offending post needs to be removed. Recrimination and the blame game can all be played at a later stage. The anger parents feel is completely understandable and can certainly be used as energy to ensure that certain strategies and initiatives are introduced so as to help your child to recover. However, the meeting between the parents needs a more focused and clear approach; don't get side-tracked!

An authentic yet compassionate approach is probably the most effective when addressing the offender's parents, as the authenticity offered will show the pain you feel and the compassion will help build bridges. Don't accuse – explain. As you are accusing the parents' child, 'I' statements should be used when meeting the offender's parents – 'I hope that we can get over this ...' 'I felt very distressed when I saw how upset my daughter was ...', 'I want to sort this out positively ...' – because as soon as the target's parents fall into 'you' statements, they will probably quickly become accusatory. It is more helpful to explain how you feel without accusing the other family of being insensitive louts. This takes practice and isn't learned overnight but it can be a great way to maintain civil relationships when you are utterly furious.

How to identify the bully's motivations

Michelle Obama's advice, 'When they go low, you go high' is inspiring stuff indeed and it is a good message to tell your children. If you can figure out the bully's modus operandi and if you can explain to your child what seems to be happening in age-appropriate language, then you can show your child how to take the high road.

For some scenarios, especially if your child is still quite young, you can set your child a challenge: every time the potential bully makes a nasty comment, then your child can try to kill the situation with kindness. Sometimes this won't be appropriate at all and it is up to the parents to identify exactly what is happening. But if the situation can be relieved by your child taking the high road, it can be a good life lesson. The parent can promise to give their child a treat any time they manage to take the high road and, hopefully, after a while the child will realise the benefits of killing with kindness.

It's important to figure out what is driving the bully's behaviour. Maybe the bullies are snobs or shallow or perhaps they are chronically dissatisfied or even being bullied themselves? This requires analysis and tentative exploration as pinpointing an incorrect motivation can send everyone off down the wrong road. Beware of simplistic explanations as they rarely explain the whole picture.

Perhaps the bully is jealous – but they may also be irritated, competitive and determined to get the better of the target. In a scenario such as this, it would be helpful to identify exactly what they are jealous of (e.g. the target's good looks) and what is irritating them (e.g. the target is over-confident) and how they are trying to get the better of them (e.g. trying to take the target down a peg or two by posting ugly pics).

The offender's weakness might be their vanity, and the target might appeal to this by posting some nice pics of him or her, or by complimenting a jacket he or she wears. Of course, very few worthwhile things in life are either simple or easy, and a couple of compliments won't stop a concerted bullying campaign – it might, however, nip a growing hostility in the bud, especially if it is followed up with other clever boxing.

How to develop emotional intelligence

If you wish to look after your child's well-being, then developing their emotional intelligence is the most beneficial approach to take. It will take some time to see the rewards, however; as the song tells us, you need to 'Keep your eyes on the prize, Hold on'. Emotional intelligence can be described as the ability to understand, manage and effectively express feelings, as well as being able to engage and navigate successfully with those of others. Emotional intelligence is very beneficial in this world; for example, according to *Psychology Today*, 90% of high performers in the workplace possess high EQ, while 80% of low performers have low EQ.[49] Unlike IQ, which seldom changes significantly over time, emotional intelligence can evolve and increase with our desire to develop.

Teaching emotional intelligence in children

✓ **Teach your children how to manage negative emotions.** To help manage their emotions, children need to learn how to reduce 'negative personalisation' and to reduce the fear of rejection. If your child has been left out of a fun social outing there are generally multiple ways of viewing the situation before reacting. If you or your child tend to personalise behaviour negatively, you will automatically assume that it is because your child has been expressly rejected. Yet, if you look at it another way, perhaps there was another reason for the so-called rejection — for example, maybe a parent owed another parent a favour and so took certain kids — and not your child — to the cinema. People do what they do because of themselves more than because of us. Parents can teach their children to widen their perspective on any given situation. Children can learn to manage their fear of negative emotions by being provided with multiple options in important situations so that no matter what happens, there is a strong possibility that they will cope just fine. For example, if your child plans to go to the local disco with a Queen Bee who has a history of suddenly letting your child down at the last minute, make sure your child has a viable Plan B ready to use if needed.

✓ **Explain the concept of self-regulation.** Parents need to build self-awareness in their children so that they can become good at recognising their emotions building up. When children can become good at recognising and understanding other people's emotions then they can anticipate behaviour and respond accordingly. The sooner children are made aware that we all have positive and negative feelings, the sooner they can accept that they may have dark feelings about a person but they do not have to act upon them. Learning to regulate emotions is a key aspect of emotional well-being and so it is a gift parents can bestow upon their children. This can be done slowly by empathising with your child, 'I can see you're upset', and then provoking the child to consider their options, 'I wonder would it help you if you had some time on your own in your bedroom/had a shower/listened to some music?'

✓ **Teach your children how to tolerate distress.** The seminal writer Andrew Solomon tells us that 'we cannot bear a pointless torment, but we can endure great pain if we believe that it's purposeful'. It will be easier for your child to learn to tolerate distress if you can help them find some meaning or purpose in their pain — even the lesson that sometimes people are difficult can help a person make sense out of pain. The important aspect of this is that parents can help their children 'forge meaning' from any situation — the lesson may not be obvious but, with some insight, it can help make us better people.[50] We all experience some distress in our lives and so parents need to teach their children the difference between being assertive and being reactive. If children are becoming stressed, it is helpful to ask them to put some cold water on their face and bring them out into the fresh air, because cool temperatures help reduce our anxiety levels. As the saying goes, 'Motion dictates emotion', and aerobic exercises, such as going for a walk or running down a hill, reduce fear and depression. Validating your child's emotions without becoming worked up yourself is key to teaching your child the ability to tolerate distress. This might mean saying seemingly bland but necessarily heartfelt sentences such as, 'I can see that you're very disappointed; it must be very hard on you.' While it is very hard for parents to see their children in pain and not be able to take the pain away, they are necessary emotions that everyone experiences if they are to grow and develop. Authentic connection can often have more value at this time for teenagers than their parents charging in with some trite reassurances that they will 'sort it'.

✓ **Guide your children towards flexibility in times of adversity.** Flexible thinking is the cornerstone to well-adjusted behaviour and the more your child is prone to rigid thinking, the more difficult it will be to find solutions to complex problems. There is no one solution to life; every problem needs to be examined and an adaptable mentality will fix an issue sooner than rigid, black and white thinking. There is more than one way to skin a cat and so each time a hoped-for solution fails then other solutions should be examined.

✓ **Teach resilience.** Life is often difficult and if children can learn to bounce back from adversity they will be well equipped to face down the slings and arrows of outrageous fortune. With every challenging encounter, parents can ask their children, 'What can you learn from this experience?' and 'What is the real priority here?' and 'If you think outside the box, what are some other options?' The higher the quality of the question, the higher the quality of the answer you can expect. Constructive and penetrating questions help kids to gain a proper perspective so that they can learn to bounce back from difficult situations.

✓ **Provoke thought and consideration.** 'Socratic questions' are open-ended questions that challenge mindless thought processes and provoke further thought and consideration. The parent might at first ask, 'I wonder what was happening that the [attacker] decided to do that?' or 'I wonder what they will do the next time they see you?' It is a slow and thoughtful process and the questions can be asked at many different occasions and in many different ways.

✓ **Show your children how to remain proactive instead of reactive.** As Jean-Paul Sartre tells us, 'Hell is other people', and whether at home, in work or at school, unreasonable people are everywhere. Taking some time out, deep breaths and counting slowly to ten can work to slow down our immediate reactive response and harness a more helpful response. It can often be very healing for the target when they realise that the bully's behaviour is mostly about the bully and less about the target.

✓ **Speculate about strangers.** Speculating about how others are feeling when you are out and about is the easiest way to teach empathic understanding and build emotional intelligence. When you are in the shops or in a café and see someone acting oddly or out of turn, encourage your child to speculate about what might be going on for the person. Show them how to put yourself in someone else's shoes, demonstrate how you read strangers' behaviour through their body language, their tone of voice and their facial expressions. If you have a difficult relative show them how to better understand what it is that motivates the relative to behave in an awkward manner. If empathic understanding is not your strength, then ensure there is someone in your child's life — an aunt, a cousin or a counsellor — who can be entrusted to help your child with this.

✓ **Try to understand famous people.** Parents can teach their children better social skills simply by watching shows like *Britain's Got Talent* on TV with them and wondering aloud what it must be like to be on this reality show. Celebrities such as Kim Kardashian or Ed Sheeran can also be analysed in a bid to better understand human nature. It doesn't matter who your child analyses — the point is that they try to cultivate a better understanding of human nature. If you can find individuals your children are interested in — sports stars, celebrities or actors — it will then be easier to engage your children's interest. If they dismiss this with a complete lack of interest or understanding, then this is a sign that parents need to put more effort into building their child's understanding of human nature.

✓ **Teach your children how to express intimate emotions in an appropriate manner.** This is essential for maintaining and establishing close personal relationships. There are millions of ways that communicate, 'I care about you' and these communications are essential to maintaining happy relationships. If your child is OTT with their BFF they can become possessive and jealous. It is up to the parents to gently guide their child towards a better way of communicating love and friendship.

✓ **Discuss TV shows.** Discuss whether people in soap operas or comedies would really act like this in real life; what is destructive about each character's behaviour; what they could have done instead and what choices they have. Make sure your child understands 'stop signals'. Some children push their way well past the normal boundaries of good behaviour. These kids need to be taught how to read the signals better.

✓ **Try out role-playing.** Imaginative role-playing can be a very effective method to develop social skills — young children already do this. Children who enjoy drama can really run with this ball and add to their knowledge of human nature through amateur dramatics. The 'empty chair technique' is a popular strategy that many psychotherapists use in a bid to engage a client's feelings, thoughts and behaviour as the client gives the imaginary person in the chair a piece of their mind without fear of repercussion. If the target is attending counselling, they might find this technique both satisfying and revelatory.

✓ **Consider your speech patterns.** The kind of language we use is crucial to teach our children how to communicate effectively. How do you describe others? Are you judgemental or tolerant? If you choose to comment on behaviour with comments akin to 'He is a pig,' 'She is selfish,' 'He is such a bully', then you are not using helpful communication because you are labelling the person instead of attempting to recognise the emotions behind the behaviour. It is more effective to try to delve a bit deeper into the situation with comments like, 'I wonder what happened for that person to act so meanly?' 'Do you think that child who is crying might be hungry or tired?' ' I wonder would she act differently if she felt better about herself?' Our children model their behaviour on their parents' behaviour — often choosing to exactly replicate it or else react against it. If you are judgemental and show little understanding or interest in why people behave in a certain way then it is unlikely that either you (or your children) have developed much empathy or indeed, social skills.

✓ **Discuss stories that are in the news.** Parents can lead children to explore the news stories and to analyse the different emotions that the people involved might be feeling — for example, Hillary Clinton's bid for presidency is a good story with plenty of complicated emotions involved. If we talk about all the different highs and lows that people experience in public life then we are teaching our children that we need to be resilient if we are to succeed at anything.

✓ **Teach the art of diplomatic assertiveness.** Teaching your children how to become assertive without being aggressive will take time. Learning to set down appropriate boundaries is an essential life lesson so that our children can grow up to be successfully functioning adults. This includes learning how to disagree without being disagreeable, saying no without feeling guilty and protecting ourselves from anyone taking advantage of us. Just like adults, children need to learn to avoid beginning sentences with 'you' and focus on sentences beginning with 'I' because 'you' sounds combative and accusatory, while 'I' is empowering. Children also need to be taught how to say 'no' effectively, courteously and without apology or excuses. Parents can help their children to access their strong voice in order to stand strong against bullying; they can teach them to look people in the eye and say 'No' in a strong and low voice that gives meaning and challenge. Parents can also show their children how to practise their posture and their body language so they can tap into their inner strength. For some people, this is a lifelong lesson that has to be revisited again and again, and yet, awareness of their ability to say 'No' can in itself free children from becoming doormats.

✓ **Increase empathic understanding.** Some people are naturally empathic. Others are not. But empathy can be increased. Teaching empathy will give children more profound understanding, more compassion, teach them to be able to handle bullying and to refrain from being a bully. Empathy operates on the same neural pathway as forgiveness and it fosters more trust, cooperation, and better relationships. Teaching empathy helps children to understand the feelings behind the behaviour. Putting yourself in the difficult person's shoes with a display of empathy can also slow down reactive responses and can be beneficial to calming a troubled mind. Although empathy doesn't excuse unacceptable behaviour, it does allow us to better realise that behaviour often says more about the person behaving than it says about the recipient of the behaviour.

✓ **Be kind to yourself and be kind to others.** Jon Kabat-Zinn, the founder of mindfulness-based stress reduction, advises us to become 'a compassionate mess'. If we can acknowledge and be compassionate about our fallibility, then we won't have a need to play the victim as we will have licked our wounds adequately and given ourselves the appropriate attention when we needed tender, loving care.

How to help children adapt to their environment

Neither you nor your child can control how others act, but children *can* learn how to adapt to their environment and control how they respond to situations. Indeed, in certain predatory environments, it is *essential* that your child learns to adapt to their current situation.

During the early, formative years of a child's development parents are supposed to groom and train them about different social signals and how they should respond to them. This might begin with teaching your toddler how to play nicely, how to share and why we don't whack other people over the head. As children grow older, these social cues become more nuanced and children also begin to lean on friends and peers as sources for useful social skills.

This is not to say that the child should learn to run with the hare and hunt with the hounds; some children (and adults) are universally liked and some aren't. Some of us, while worthwhile in our own right, just don't have the conventional qualities that are required for popularity; we might be passionate, intense, honest and loyal and we might have lots of worthwhile attributes to offer the world – and yet we can still be unpopular. I know that my own intensity, passion and honesty are incredibly annoying for some people and they go out of their way to avoid me – but then I'm 42 years old and I have accepted that these people are not my tribe. It was much more difficult to accept this when I was 14 years old.

Just because a person doesn't have the traits that make them popular doesn't mean they have less to offer – often they might have more to offer – but it does mean that they might find it difficult to handle school and might then run into negative relationships during the intensely social teenage years.

Perhaps your child is socially awkward, hopelessly naive or painfully tactless? Perhaps your child doesn't understand the signals that are being communicated by their peers? Perhaps the bullying has been building for a long time and you always hoped it would go away? The details are just the elements that distinguish your child's experience of bullying from another child's. The bullies have targeted your child because, for some reason, they can. They have identified something in your child's make-up that they consider weak or inferior and they enjoy the thrill of power they feel by highlighting this weakness.

Perhaps your child shouldn't change one iota of their personality or perhaps they need to be more sensitive to their environment? These are big questions and ultimately they are personal decisions that are up to the child and the parent. However, if a child or parent decides to stand up for their right to be different, in certain environments they can expect to have some negative reactions.

The cold, hard, bitter pill that you and your child may have to swallow is that, in certain circumstances, it may be more beneficial to your child to adapt to the environment. In some situations, asking the bullies to modify their behaviour is pie in the sky – it just ain't gonna happen. And in the meantime, if you're not careful, your child's self-esteem will become crushed. If your child can learn to accept that there is a malignant force at play here and sometimes it is better to box clever than to be knocked out, then you can help your child identify the most appropriate action.

It may sound trite, but it's actually very important: sometimes the parent need to help their children to find their tribe. If a child feels like a freak in school but has a sound base of friends outside school, then they are much more likely to be able to handle the bullying. The parent, with some flexible thinking and a commitment to finding a solution, can help with this.

Perhaps your teenager is into anime. Well, find an anime convention that they can attend. If music is their thing then buy them tickets to concerts, ensure they take up music lessons or perhaps learn about music production. Instead of allowing your teenager to exist in a vacuum that makes them feel like a social outcast, give your child the chance to grow in their social abilities with a sympathetic crowd – not the hostile crowd who are bullies and bystanders – but with a crowd who have similar interests. It is important that these activities involve face-to-face socialisation – online video games don't cut it (no matter what your teen tells you!).

Sometimes, children have little choice in their social circles. I know when I was growing up I was pretty much forced to be friends with all the kids on the road – it was either that or be a social outcast; there was no middle road. If your teenager or pre-teen is stuck in a similar situation, perhaps you can ensure that they retain links with old friends from outside the neighbourhood or else that they get opportunities to make new friends in different environments. And as the (hopefully) more emotionally intelligent adult, it is important that you help them to maintain these friendships as they may need them when they hit choppy waters and feel inadequate and insecure among their peers.

How to deal with violent bullying

Parents can explore the 'use of force continuum' with your child. The use of force continuum is a standard used by civilians and law enforcement agents to give guidelines as to what level of force is acceptable if you are attacked. As a psychotherapist I will always err on the side of trying to talk things out but, if I am mugged on a lonely street without any potential of calming my aggressor down or appealing to passers-by, then I am willing to use force to ensure that I stay alive.

The leading clinical psychologist David Coleman also questions why one child should be required to accept another child's dominance.

In my experience, and the experience of many of the youngsters that I have worked with, if an initial physical attack is not met with some degree of physical response, then it tends to happen again. If another child discovers that they can push someone around, they often continue to do so. In most cases, if a physical attack leads to a physical response, like a shove, or a thump, it may develop into a full-blown fight, but that then tends to be the end of it. There is rarely a 'second go'. The attacker thinks twice about picking on a child who fights back because it requires so much more effort. It is easier to just move on to a different child who may be an easier target. Whereas if a child submits to the initial assault, be it a shove, a kick, or a thump, then they are at much greater risk of receiving another the next day, and for as long as the attacker chooses. By not fighting back they give a very clear message that they will not resist. They give an equally clear message that they accept the other child's dominance.[51]

As Coleman points out, children, just like adults, have the right to defend themselves. If a potential aggressor is violently bullying your child, your child can learn to take a flexible response and group different responses according to the severity of the attack.

Targets also need to learn to choose their battles – sometimes one potential battle is better ignored so that the target has the psychic energy required for the real battle that will inevitably take place. A simple continuum might be:

1. Ignore the bully.

2. Tell the bully to stop.

3. Tell a responsive adult.

But a more complicated continuum could be:

1. Resist the bullies' physical attacks.

2. Use force equal to the level needed to escape from the bullies' attack.

3. Tell a responsive adult as soon as possible.

Some bullies are very cunning and they choose the time of their attack very carefully. They might isolate the target when there is no chance of anyone coming to their rescue. Your child will need to consider when and where they are being isolated or bullied and prepare themselves for action around this – they may need to ensure that they are not alone in certain places while they are undertaking more long-term bully-proofing.

Bullies don't like the taste of their own medicine – they specifically prey on the weak so that they can feel powerful. If the target can manage to threaten the bully's power without showing weakness, most bullies will move on to easier prey.

Although I am not advocating violence, I am advocating self-defence. A child who is likely to be faced with a violent attack needs to know how to avoid violence, how to talk people down, how to distract – but also, if necessary, when it might be appropriate to use violence, to defend themselves. If you acknowledge and understand this, you engage in the morality of the issue better than someone who pretends they would never use force but then suddenly fights back when they themselves are mugged. Perhaps parents can discuss with their children when it might be appropriate to fight back in self-defence and how they can ensure that they have enough self-control to stop when they no longer need to fight.

For some people the continuum of force is completely useless as they are physically much weaker than the bullies. Yet Paul McGrath, the former Irish footballer, had an interesting insight into the bullying he experienced when he was growing up in an orphanage in Dublin in the 1950s. Speaking on the *Miriam O'Callaghan Show* on RTÉ Radio 1, Paul McGrath pointed out that the bullies soon came to know that no matter how big they were, they wouldn't get away with bullying him without being on the receiving end of a few digs themselves. 'If you called me something, it's *on* …. He [the bully] might be someone that I knew that could beat me but I would still run him. He might leave me on the ground saying maybe that was a bad idea …'[52] So McGrath's tactic was to hurt the bully enough so that the bully wouldn't attack him easily again – he basically made it hard work for the bully to bully him.

Many parents enrol their child in martial arts classes and, while this will be very powerful in helping the child in future years, it won't take effect soon enough for the bullying that is taking place today and so, in the meantime, the child will also need to be taught how to box clever; they will need to learn to appeal to potential upstanders, seek responsive adults and access their inner power and emotional intelligence. However, it is interesting to note that the physically weaker will often awaken more upstanding emotions in others than a more physically equal match. So the one good thing about being significantly weaker than the bullies is that the school authorities and other stronger peers are much more likely to step in to help the target (i.e. if a tiny person is being attacked by a large individual, more people are more likely to come to the aid of the target than if the target is an average-sized person).

Absolute pacifists argue that all violence is wrong and should never be conducted, even in self-defence. However, although these aspirations are noble, many of us have such keenly developed survival instincts that we automatically react to an attack. 'Relative pacifists' are perhaps more understanding of our animal nature and argue that violence, although always undesirable, can be an option of last resort. Our self-esteem is fragile and it is important we learn to respect our boundaries as we move through life. Not only that, bullies can't be allowed to take over every situation and it could be deemed an altruistic action to ensure bullies are given firm boundaries!

So the jury is out. Yes, it might be better if we could all locate our inner nobility and invite the bully, as Jesus Christ did, to hit us on the other cheek, to take our cloak as well and to generally walk all over us – but then it might not be very good for either the bully or society if we allow bullies to trample on us.

It's not what happens, it's how you react to it that matters. The stoic philosopher Epictetus was born a slave in AD 35 and subsequently banished from Rome. Epictetus lived a very difficult life; not only was he born a slave but he was also crippled. Yet Epictetus was a philosopher and his stoic philosophy became a way of life for him. To Epictetus, although events might be beyond our control, we should accept whatever happens to us calmly and dispassionately. According to Epictetus, we are responsible for our own actions and we can choose how we respond to any event.

How a target responds to nasty incidents can have a profound impact on the situation. If the child can pre-identify what reaction is the most effective action then they will be ready for the next attack. However, all plans should have a contingency plan and there should always be an option to walk away so that they can live to fight another day. The following responses can help your child to gauge what they think will be the most likely scenario in their power play:

- If the target responds by standing up to the bullies and winning the confrontation the bullies will probably move on to easier targets (but, depending on the circumstances, the bullies may plot to exact revenge one day).

- If the target responds by accessing strong long-term support from responsive adults, the environment can change in a comprehensive and positive way.

- If the target responds by calling for and receiving back-up then the potential bullies might move on to easier prey or they might channel their destructive tendencies in another way.

- If the target responds by standing up to the bullies and loses the confrontation, the bullies will be re-energised and more dangerous.

- If the target calls for back-up but doesn't receive support then the bullies will be re-energised and may quickly ratchet the bullying up a few notches.

- If the target responds with high emotion and dramatic behaviour the bullies might be highly entertained by this and continue to return again and again looking for further entertainment.

- If the target responds by enduring the bullying quietly then the bullies may continue to bully mindlessly but, over time, as boredom sets in, the bullying may go up a gear every so often.

How to support your child during bullying

This needs to be communicated in both actions and words. You might need to confront the bullies or the school to show your solidarity, or you might just need to provide them with things to look forward to – for example, maybe you could finally allow them to have a much-longed-for pet. You might also need to seriously discuss the possibility of changing schools to show that you are truly standing shoulder-to-shoulder with them. Feelings of abandonment and utter loneliness can be very intense for the bullied target, and parents need to be sensitive to these feelings. What matters most is that your child is made to understand that you are standing behind them and you are ready to take whatever action that might be helpful.

Be very careful about keeping your child's privacy or confidence if this is appropriate. Sometimes it won't be appropriate, but if you have to break a confidence, try to do it very carefully and sensitively – and it might be important to tell your child beforehand that you are forced to break their confidence for a specific reason.

Parents can make the child's home – or certain rooms in the home – a haven from the bullying. Putting some time and effort into making life gentle and kind at home so that there can be a sense of relief sometimes can communicate your solidarity to your child. Sometimes it might be helpful for your child to help design a nice place for them to hang out, or you could update their room. Buy them some comfy cushions or special lighting to set the scene and show that you wish to make life easier for them.

Some rooms in the house could be designated tech-free rooms so that cyberbullies can't stalk them every moment of the day. Similarly, some times of the day – perhaps between 4 p.m. and

6 p.m. – could be deemed tech-free as then your child will have a chance to calm down after the school experience.

While some kids need extra support through counselling, other kids benefit more from meeting up with old friends or forgetting about their worries while they indulge in their hobbies. Still others will benefit from learning certain social skills and assertiveness from books or films. Some kids will want a kind teacher to keep an eye out for them and to give them some jobs to complete during lunchtime, while other kids will be devastated if the teachers are involved. The 'one important character' in a person's life can have a huge impact and so it might be helpful for your child if you can identify a sympathetic teacher or supervising adult who is prepared to go the extra mile for your child when you aren't available. Of course, different strokes work for different folks; each child will have their own unique needs and so long as their parents are attuned to their child's specific emotional needs, the child should be OK.

It is important for parents to be aware that many teenagers who have been bullied simply cannot bring themselves to discuss the shame and the humiliation with a counsellor or with anyone else. Not only that, but many middle-aged men and women who come to me for counselling still find it difficult to expose their vulnerabilities even 20 and 30 years later. Although as a psychotherapist I generally agree that 'it's good to talk', sometimes talking about the specifics of the bullying causes so much distress that it can be much more helpful for parents to be sensitive to their child's feelings and allow them to focus on how best to come through this experience with their sense of self intact and perhaps some improved emotional intelligence instead of discussing the humiliating specifics of the story.

Support can come in many different ways. Appropriate books such as Louise O'Neill's *Asking For It* or William Golding's *Lord of the Flies* can show teenagers how nasty kids can be when they are vying for a place in the pecking order (more books are suggested in the resources at the back of the book). Some teenagers will benefit from being introduced to appropriate forums with other teenagers who are also being bullied (parents should research these before proposing specific sites) while others will benefit from writing in a journal.

More than any other trait, self-acceptance is the one that will most likely help your child to stand their sacred ground when it comes to bullying. If the parents can show, through modelling, how to accept yourself, how to accept your body and your personality, and how to accept others – flaws and all – they will then lead their children to accept themselves and also to accept others as they are and not as they hope to be. Parents can help their teens or tweens become more aware of their strengths and weaknesses so that they can begin to try to accept themselves. Self and other acceptance is no minor event – indeed most of us are in our 40s before we manage to acquire some self-acceptance and yet if the parent can put their child on the road to beginning to learn to accept themselves, it is a powerful gift.

Positive reinforcement is also essential if the child is to believe they are worthy. Maybe the child is studious, kind and sweet or maybe they are quick to anger but also quick to laugh. The child's positive qualities need to be celebrated and negative qualities accepted with compassionate tenderness. Consider finding a mantra such as 'You're a lovely, kind and gentle person' repeated so often that it enters the child's bones; the mantra 'don't be so hard on yourself and don't be so hard on others' can also be effective to cultivate well-being and a forgiving nature. Make sure your child believes that you have confidence in them and make sure the mantra you choose is appropriate to them – nobody feels great if someone tells them a pack of lies, e.g. telling your child that they are popular when they have no friends will merely accentuate the child's feelings of isolation. It's no use – and often destructive – giving the child imagined strengths while missing their real strengths.

When the bullying is over, continue to be ready to nip things in the bud if needs be. Oftentimes the bullying can go away because the bullies realise that if they don't back off they will bring trouble on their shoulders. But they might be furious with the outcome and determined to get back at the target in the long term. The concerned parents need to keep an eye out for this situation to rear its ugly head weeks or even months after it has all died down. It might start in a light manner and your child might be given to a victim mentality, exaggerating because they have been so hurt in the past, and so the parent will need to exercise a lot of emotional intelligence when figuring out the lie of the land. If the bullying does begin to return, the parent and target should act as soon as possible so as to nip it in the bud. Bullying is a huge experience and your child won't be able to spring back to being the way they were before the experience but, as explained in the next chapter, this doesn't mean that hope is lost; it may make them stronger and more powerful than ever before.

9

Recovering from bullying
Stronger than ever before

*'You either get bitter or you get better. It's that simple. You either
take what has been dealt to you and allow it to make you a
better person, or you allow it to tear you down. The choice
does not belong to fate. It belongs to you.'*

Josh Shipp

Once your child has experienced serious bullying, everything
has changed. Your child won't go back to the way they were
before – they may emerge battered and bruised but wiser
and stronger, or they may emerge battered, bruised and feeling
defeated and overwhelmed by the world – but, no matter what,
they will be changed by their experiences. It is the parent's role to
help support and guide their child through difficult experiences.
We can't take the hits for our children, but we can do something far
more powerful and far more helpful – we can show them *how* to
take the hits so that they can emerge a wiser and stronger person
who is better equipped to deal with the world.

Living well is the best revenge

There is something incredibly satisfying about hearing the stories
of targets who rose out of the ashes of their distress to find fame and

fortune. Steven Spielberg was called 'a dirty Jew'. The girls in Miley Cyrus's school formed an 'Anti-Miley Club'. Rihanna was mocked for not being 'black enough'. Eminem was bullied so severely that he ended up in hospital with a concussion and temporary blindness. Howard Stern learned judo to defend himself against bullying. And all of them not only survived, but thrived.

Indeed, there are so many stories of famous people who have been bullied that it is arguable that the trauma they suffered fostered a resilience and single-mindedness that spurred these celebrities on to greatness. According to the British psychotherapist and paediatric counsellor Julia Samuel, 'Research shows that, given the right support, there is a thing called post-traumatic growth. If you can find a way of navigating the loss, then it does change your perception of yourself and you realise that you can survive anything.'[53]

The *Mad Men* star Christina Hendricks grew up feeling 'ugly, awkward and horrible'. She described her experiences at school as 'like something out of *Lord of the Flies*'. According to Hendricks, she 'had the worst high school experience ever. I went to a very mean school and was bullied like crazy … If I could go back and tell my 14-year-old self anything, it would be: "Don't worry. You're going to be doing exactly what you want to be doing in 20 years, and those a***holes are still going to be a***holes. So let it go!"' Interestingly, Hendricks recalled that 'instead of breaking down and conforming, I stood firm. That is probably why I was unhappy.'[54] Winona Ryder also had a feisty approach to her bullies. Winona was asked to leave her school even though it was she who had been bullied, and the bullies were allowed to remain. 'Years later I went into a coffee shop and I ran into one of the girls who'd kicked me, and she said "Winona, Winona, can I have your autograph?" And I said, "Do you remember me? Remember in seventh grade you beat up that kid?" And she said. "Kind of." And I said, "That was me. Go f**k yourself."'

The Olympic superstar Michael Phelps was also bullied as a child. This time, the so-called issue was that Phelps had big ears and a lisp when he was a child. 'It's kind of crazy. When I go up around where I used to live [in Baltimore], you still see the same people who were picking on me. They're still around, bussing tables or whatever, probably still acting the same way. They'll try to talk to me and I'm thinking, "Yeah, why are you talking to me now? You were picking on me then."'

The list of celebrities who were bullied goes on and on. It comes as little surprise that someone as distinctive as Lady Gaga didn't quite fit in with the strict conventionality of school, as she remarked on the *Ellen DeGeneres Show*, 'I didn't fit in at high school, I wanted to be like Boy George and I felt like a freak. It took me a long time for me to be OK with myself.'

Jackie Chan was also bullied in school until one day he stood up for another boy. 'I was bullied quite a lot when I was growing up in my Peking Opera School. I allowed myself to be bullied because I was scared and didn't know how to defend myself. I was bullied until I prevented a new student from being bullied. By standing up for him, I learned to stand up for myself.'

Victoria Beckham too was severely bullied at school. 'The [bullies] were literally picking things up out of puddles and throwing them at me, and I just stood there on my own. No one was with me. I didn't have any friends. People would push me around, say they were going to beat me up after school, chase me. It was miserable, my whole schooling, miserable. I tried to be friends with people, but I didn't fit in. So I kept myself to myself.'

Even cutie Justin Timberlake was bullied. Timberlake also described the experience on the *Ellen DeGeneres Show*: 'I grew up in Tennessee, and if you didn't play football, you were a sissy. I got slurs all the time because I was in music and art. But everything that you get picked on for is essentially what's going to make you sexy as an adult.' Perhaps the difference for Justin Timberlake was that he had a mother who encouraged him to have pride in his difference. 'Growing up in school, no one ever called me anything close to an innovator, they called me different, they called me weird, they called me a couple of other words I can't say on TV. So thankfully my mother taught me that being different was a good thing; that being different meant you could actually make a difference.'

Stories like these need to be drummed into our children as they grow up so they know that when they are going through a difficult time, they can rise again. It is also helpful if parents instil in their children (before any bullying has taken place) that the best revenge to almost any situation is living well. This will encourage your child to protect their happiness before they decide to sink to the cynicism of their aggressors.

The poet Maya Angelou points out that, 'We delight in the beauty of the butterfly, but rarely admit the changes it has gone through to achieve that beauty.' But bullied kids need to learn about the troubles others have gone through before they reached success so that they know that they too can emerge like a gloriously beautiful butterfly.

Karl is a stylish 24-year-old who is positively evangelical about his experience of school life. Karl knew that he was gay from an early age and he was accepting of his tendency to be quite feminine. This was all fine in the early years of his life. However, when he reached puberty, other boys in his class began to call him 'Queenie'. This didn't particularly bother Karl and so he let it go. When he moved to second level, the mild taunting took a turn for the worse and Karl was beaten up after being accused of eyeing up another boy in the toilets. 'I honestly couldn't have had less interest in that horrible brute, but they all thought I was a screaming queen, desperate for any passing glimpse of a urinating penis. I was never actually that desperate.'

From that day on, the bullies began to target Karl and he was often assaulted during school and taunted on social media after school hours. Luckily for Karl, his parents were quite political and when his mother showed him a movie about Malcolm X, Karl's life was suddenly transformed. Karl decided to set up an LGTBQ group in school and invited past pupils to come and speak about what it was like to be gay in that school. Karl also started an initiative that provided worry boxes all over the school and held regular meetings with year heads to identify some troubling issues — and students — that needed nipping in the bud.

Karl is now a youth worker and advocate for teenagers and he helps teenagers come to terms with their sexuality and gender. He feels that in many ways his bullying experience was quite positive for him as it gave him some insight into how difficult it is for many people to accept difference and it also led him to the path that he is now on.

When a person has gone through bullying or felt the complicated emotions of experiencing difficult and hurtful relationships, it is all too easy to become embittered and cynical. Those kids who never learned how to handle the bullies can often go on to be a target for future bullies, and so it is essential that parents guide their children to positively manage the situation. It might be through counselling or through reading or as a result of other approaches, but it is crucial that the target of bullying or exclusion emerges from the experience with a better understanding of human nature.

The following attributes can come about as a direct consequence of bullying and so if you, as a parent, can see how bullying has damaged your child, perhaps it is time for you to cultivate these attributes in your child so the damage can begin to heal.

Increased inner strength

Perhaps the most important thing a parent can bestow upon their bullied child is the ability to tap into their inner power. It can be difficult for some children to access their power and so this must be handled sensitively – there is little point in telling a bullied child that their power is within them and off they go – it's a much more complicated process than that.

When the child is bullied, the time is now – suddenly, urgently, the time is upon the parent to teach their child how to tap into their inner power. A lot of parents worry that their children simply don't have very much inner strength, but every animal has some instinct for self-preservation and it is this instinct that parents need to help their children identify and use to their advantage. There are a whole range of approaches that a person can take to get the better of the bullies – this is certainly not a one-size-fits-all situation – so it can be very helpful for the child to figure out what their inner strength is and how they can best use it.

Often you will see your child's power and strength at home among their siblings or parents – they might be sarcastic, witty or they might get very angry and take over a situation with determination when their blood is up. It doesn't matter how the strength emerges, the point is that the parent needs to be able to notice when the child is powerful (even if it is only in front of their baby sister), because then it is inarguable that they have inner power and strength of mind.

From this point on it is up to the parent and child to figure out how to move beyond the front door with this power. Showing your strength out in the big, bad world can be quite a challenge for some people, but the more the parent identifies the child's inner power at home, the more the child will become accustomed to perceiving themselves as having some power that can be one day unleashed.

The parent can give their child the opportunity to access their inner strength with baby steps at first. If they are imprisoned by shyness around strangers, then initially you could ask them to order for themselves in a restaurant, and over time you might build up to ordering something that isn't on the menu or asking for more potatoes. Eventually, if the opportunity arises, they could complain about a dish. The point is that Rome wasn't built in a day and parents have to realise that if a certain tendency in their child is holding them back then it is important to help them to work on this so that their children learn to honour their feelings.

The gift of resilience

Once an individual has acquired the gift of resilience, they are ready for almost anything. At the heart of resilience is the belief that you can cope with whatever life throws at you. Resilience is both empowering and comforting. If parents can guide their child through a bullying experience so they emerge intact and emotionally aware then the child will have learned resilience. Kenneth Ginsburg in *Building Resilience in Children and Teens* tells us:

> *When children become responsible for their own decisions and actions, they learn to face joyful and disappointing results. They learn that mistakes happen; sometimes they could have prevented them, but the next time they will be more prepared for them. If they are given many chances to exercise control in their lives, they are far less likely to see themselves as passive victims and blame others. This is the core of resilience – when faced with adversity, failure, or stress, kids who have a true center of control will be able to bounce back. Ultimately they will be happier, more optimistic, and better equipped to face the next challenge.*[55]

Improved emotional intelligence

If a child is properly supported by their parents during a bullying experience, they will have learned how to adapt more successfully to their specific social environment. This will make them more sensitive to the social mores of the culture that they may grow up to reject or accept in the future. When they leave school they may be sufficiently angered and motivated by this experience to make the world a better and more accepting place. However, until then, they will be more sensitive and socially aware of their specific environment.

If a child has special needs and their lack of social skills is the crux of the problem, then perhaps the child can be taught to improve their social skills by learning to anticipate problems arising and to ask for help in good time from appropriate people. This might mean that you, as a parent, might need to become your child's advocate in certain settings. These sorts of thing come much more easily to some than to others, but if you learn it, it will be of benefit to you and your child for ever more.

Improved social skills and relationships

Children who have been bullied or excluded may learn to avoid certain people who can be fair-weather friends. The parents can provide their child with the opportunity to reflect upon the friendship in the comfort of their own home so the child can determine when the pain outweighs the pleasure of the friendship (see Chapter 2). Sometimes children need to learn that 'frenemies' will be kind some days but will inevitably be harsh another day, so they need to ascertain the mood of the difficult person and to keep their distance in certain situations.

Increased inner confidence

Although this person may have been forced to deal with the darker side of humanity earlier than would be recommended, they may also have a deeper sense of strength and confidence as a result of their experience. Children who have been bullied and then learned to face down the bullies and win will have begun a 'virtuous circle'.

A virtuous circle begins when an individual realises that certain approaches such as a flexible attitude, effort and determination can yield satisfying results. This can lead to the person being more prepared to use flexible thinking, effort and determination in other problems and this, in turn, can yield further satisfying results. (The opposite can also happen when a person tries very hard but for some unexamined reason they don't succeed and so a negative circle or a vicious cirle begins.) This is why it is so important to support our children in dark times so that they learn that a certain amount of effort and determination mixed with a flexible mindset can lead to a satisfactory end. This confidence bestowed upon the child will lead them to realise that they can handle the curveballs that life throws us; and so the virtuous circle continues.

Increased empathy and understanding

As Atticus Finch in *To Kill a Mocking Bird* puts it, 'You never really understand a person until you consider things from his point of view, until you climb inside of his skin and walk around in it.' Empathy involves entering into another person's world and being that person for a moment. If you have the ability to do this you will be better able to anticipate and fulfil a person's needs; you will be a better friend and a better person. The benefits of empathy are endless – it gives people a more profound understanding of others and with this knowledge they can find their place in the world more easily. There are also many professional reasons to develop empathy – good salespeople have stacks of empathy and can more easily sell a product to others as they understand what the other person wants and they can estimate how much they are willing to pay for it.

Most of us know what we mean when we speak about 'good' and 'evil'. 'Good' suggests kindness, compassion, selflessness, benevolence and altruism – qualities which usually stem from a sense of empathy. Over the years I have noticed that the strongest quality that I bring to my private psychotherapy practice is my empathy. I seem to be naturally empathic and I find it relatively easy to feel how it is to walk in another person's shoes. Interestingly, my husband is a very kind and good man, but he doesn't seem to have a lorry-load of empathy (luckily, he is a builder and doesn't need empathy to be good at his job). He just can't imagine how certain events could impact others, and so he can sometimes be guilty of acting in a way that could be considered selfish. Yet, when questioned (and by God, he is often questioned by yours truly) and when the situation is explained to him, he will always take the high road – probably more often than I do. My naturally unempathic husband has learned that even though he isn't naturally empathic, there are often emotional undercurrents which he may not have considered and it behoves him to wait and explore the situation before acting. He has also learned to discuss how his actions or speech might impact others before he makes a decision.

And so, on this little anecdote alone, we can't write off people who don't have empathy as 'evil' – as Jesus Christ said, 'Father, forgive them, for they know not what they are doing'. Some people can't imagine how other people feel and so they may ride roughshod over them without any idea of the destruction they are causing but, with some information and education, these people can be taught to behave better and understand more.

As a facilitator of bullying workshops I have always found it particularly satisfying to see people without empathy beginning to learn how to understand other people. We all prefer to keep bullying simple – the bully is in the wrong and the victim is in the right. But as with all issues involving human nature, it is rarely as simple as this. Bullying is a complex issue. Many bullies don't realise the damage they are causing to their victims – you see, they haven't got enough empathy to figure this out. And in turn, many targets of bullies don't understand why they are being targeted – they, in turn, haven't the insight to determine how to avoid the malevolent eye of the bully. Often both the bully and the target need to learn a greater empathic understanding of what makes us tick – the bully will be less likely to bully when they realise the hurt they are creating and the bullied will be less likely to be bullied repeatedly when they figure out how to respond effectively to bullies. Indeed, the more people understand how to behave effectively in a manner that honours themselves and honours others, the easier we will all find it to get along – and world peace will naturally ensue!

Increased moral engagement

Forty years ago, the Swedish psychologist and leading expert on bullying Dan Olweus outlined a definition of bullying that is still useful today: repeated verbal or physical harassment that involves an imbalance of power. The good news about bullying is that an estimated 75% to 90% of kids don't bully, but the bad news is that these kids are prepared to act as upstanders only 20% of the time.[56] Olweus coined the phrase 'if it's mean, intervene', and if we can convince kids to always intervene when they see bullying we can immediately reduce its frequency and intensity.

Along with the bullying, the hate crimes, the violence and the destruction, the history of humankind has some soaring flowers of hope that remind us that we have a better side, a powerful and insightful frame of reference which, with some thought, commitment and consideration, we can use to stand up to bullies. A person who has seen off the bullies has learned to dig deep beneath the underbelly of the human psyche and, having experienced this, they will naturally be *sympatico* towards others who may be going through a similar situation. Targets of bullying and exclusion can be deeper, more empathic and more self-aware as a consequence of their experiences. Bullies, especially those who have undergone a process of restorative justice, can be kinder and more morally engaged than before.

A flexible mindset

In the 1950s, the American psychologist Albert Ellis identified rigid thinking as a mindset that will lead to deep unhappiness and dysfunction. Equally, Ellis highlighted the way that a flexible mindset leads to increased likelihood of contentment. According to Ellis, rigid beliefs lead to irrational beliefs and dysfunction while less demanding, flexible beliefs lead to healthy emotions and healthy behaviour.

Today, Stanford University's Carol Dweck is the world's leading thinker on the topic of motivation. Dweck, a professor of psychology, contends that a 'growth mindset' is one of the most beneficial gifts a parent can give a child. According to Dweck, 'If parents want to give their children a gift, the best thing they can do is to teach their children to love challenges, be intrigued by mistakes, enjoy effort and keep on learning. That way, their children don't have to be slaves of praise. They will have a lifelong way to build and repair their own confidence.'[57]

Emerging from bullying as a deeper and more considered person will often bestow upon children an invaluable 'growth mindset' –

the heretofore target will have learned that their ability to grow and learn from their experiences will give them the confidence to face down other problems.

Bibliotherapy and the comfort of the arts

When parents realise that their child has been hurt by bullies or difficult friends, the anguish they feel is almost unbearable. They are ready to do anything to try to protect their children and yet sometimes, especially if the avenues of communication are shut down during the incommunicado teenage years, the best approach a parent can take is to show sympathy and take this opportunity to turn their children on to great literature, music or films.

Teenagers are at a stage developmentally where they are moving away from their parents' influence and so the arts can be a more appropriate way for their parents to connect with them than a heart-to-heart. Sometimes parents are shut out by teenagers and so they are compelled to stand helplessly by as they watch their child become wretchedly unhappy. As Alice Munro says in *Open Secrets*, 'You cannot let your parents anywhere near your real humiliations.'[58] And so, while some teenagers may tell their parents everything, many teenagers keep their deepest, darkest secrets to themselves. In situations such as these, parents could make themselves useful by finding suitable films, books or music that their teenagers might find inspiring and consoling (see the resources at the end of this book for suggestions).

When a person has been profoundly shaken by this cruel world the comfort that the arts can bring is unimaginable (personally, I don't think I could have got through my own teenage years without having Bob Dylan by my side always giving me courage).

As they grow up, children strike out on their own and find their own books, films and music, but it is important for the parents to stay connected to their children's taste so that the parent can step in at any juncture with recommendations of their own. Of course, when a child is a teenager they often have total disdain for their parent's taste, yet high art will lift even the most cynical teenager beyond their snobbery.

I was that disdainful, cynical teenager and had a lot of difficulties with my own father, yet I still remember the time he gave me a copy of Philip Larkin's poem 'This Be The Verse' one day when we were in the car together. I didn't comment and my (now passed on) father was probably very disappointed in my silent non-reaction at the time. But I read it, I understood it, and I have never forgotten it.

There are reams of poetry and art that can transcend teenage disdain and help kids who need some support. Maya Angelou's poem, 'Still I Rise' is an inspirational poem that shows how we can withstand terrible cruelty and still hold our own. Good artistic expression transcends everything and if parents can introduce their children to something special at a crucial point it can be transformative. In a similar vein, but perhaps a more overtly teen-friendly approach, is Kate Tempest's thrilling performance of 'Hold Your Own' at Glastonbury in 2015, which can be found on YouTube.

Rebuilding the parent–child bond

Far be it for me to dish out more guilt to parents – indeed, my first book, *Cotton Wool Kids*, was all about how too much pressure is being loaded on the parent's plate. But that doesn't mean that parents can lay all their problems at the door of 'the government' or 'the school'. *Cotton Wool Kids* shows how we – parents and society – need to guide our children towards mental well-being by teaching attributes that will help children's emotional health, such as increased independence, resilience and a flexible mindset.

For some reason – perhaps because parents find it such an overwhelmingly difficult problem to manage – when there's an accusation of bullying, most parents are very quick to lob the problem over to the school authorities and hope that they will sort it out. Although some schools have very effective anti-bullying policies, many schools don't, and, even with the best anti-bullying policy in the world, parents still need to step in when their child is socially isolated and consider what they can do to help.

Parents need to be prepared to give their full commitment to their child when their child is being bullied. It is not enough to inform the school and hope that they will put a stop to it. A school is mostly focused on education, and, while they will give some attention to the children's well-being, nobody will care more about your child's body and soul than you.

Almost every day I see comments online about bullying and how 'the schools are useless' and how 'something should be done', but bullying is a very complicated problem that is laden with 'he said, she said' situations. Accusations of bullying are seldom simple as there are often conflicting accounts, competing interests and complicated emotions at play. The teachers are often at a loss about what to do, and, if they can find no quick resolution, many quickly take refuge by avoiding the thorny subject and instead focus on what they are paid to do – teaching.

It amazes me that so many parents I meet seem to put the bulk of their energy into communicating with the school authorities about the bullying. But you can keep building evidence for ever. If the school is pretty useless in handling the bullying then it is very likely that it will continue to be pretty useless, and it is the parents and the child who will need to figure out the best way to resolve this difficult situation. Sometimes most of the parent's focus should be on the child and the bystander instead of the school.

If your child is being bullied, isolated or ostracised it can be the parents' opportunity to show their child the depth of their commitment and love. Although it would be better if this need didn't arise, nevertheless this is an opportunity to rebuild and reconnect with their child if they need to as it is in times of adversity that we can build deeper bonds with our loved ones.

Character development

Kindness, courage, character and empathy are the attributes the world needs if we are to reduce bullying and parents can do their bit for the world by ensuring their children are taught this as much as possible. However, that is not all. Harvard psychologist Richard Weissbourd is quoted in Emily Bazelon's seminal book on bullying, *Sticks and Stones*, as saying, 'We have a serious problem with parents' promoting the importance of happiness and achievement and demoting morality and character.' According to many leading child psychologists, this focus on happiness and achievement has had an unfortunately negative impact on children. As Weissbourd says, 'We're organizing kids around their self-esteem. But maybe the primary goal should be that kids are good people, and maybe all the focus on our own happiness doesn't actually make them happier. If you're caring for others, you're forging good and durable relationships, and there is no better path to happiness than that.'[59]

The difficult balance of guidance and support that a teenager needs is very different from the help a young child needs from their parents and yet this is the balance that parents need to aim for if they are to raise healthily functioning adults. In my book *Cotton Wool Kids* there are many examples of how heightened emotions and extraordinary effort from parents can directly lead to helpless, discontented and anxious children. It is well documented that the more independence and space a child has in real life, the less they need to socialise online. The researcher danah boyd points out that 'The more restrictions on kids' movements ... the more they use the phone and the Web to hang out.'[60] So parents must ensure their children have the independence not to rely solely upon technology for their social life, and learn to cope with problems in the shallow waters so that they can adequately face the deeper waters of adulthood.

The holistic approach

The holistic approach is effective because it focuses on engaging and developing the whole person in the treatment. Likewise, a bullying situation can benefit from a holistic approach, to ensure that all the physical, mental and social factors are taken into account so that a truly workable resolution can be found.

The primary reason that I was compelled to write this book was because there was so little practical help available for parents whose children were the targets of bullying, and it was a lack that was causing significant distress to many families. The current narrow-minded approach leads to the media regularly highlighting the 'epidemic' of bullying without providing solutions or a deeper understanding of the situation. Similarly, well-meaning people ask their friends to comment 'Amen' or some other platitude on social media in a bid to highlight the problem of bullying. However, random wringing of hands does little to help anyone; it creates alarm and tension without developing strategies to overcome the problem.

Another consequence of all this unfocused and unproductive attention upon bullying is that many people are crying bully when it isn't bullying at all. It might be a fight or a widening rift between two people, but calling it 'bullying' can turn a manageable problem into an overwhelming and bitter blame game. Recognising that conflict in relationships is a normal part of growing up is an important aspect of parental duty.

Although we can cheer and coach from the sidelines, we cannot take over our children's lives and we can't – and shouldn't – play the game of life on their behalf. Similarly, although we need to allow our children to make mistakes, it is also our job to ensure that they are not being excessively hurt and be ready to stand should-to-shoulder with them. As the musician and actor Colin Hay says, 'There is a fine line between character-building and soul-destroying', and it is the role of the parents to judge how to stay on the right side of this line.

If we as parents can help our children to develop a richer emotional vocabulary, attributes such as social skills and assertiveness can be more easily developed. This can be pivotal to helping your child emerge from teen world with their sense of self intact. Emotional intelligence can be defined as a person's ability to manage both their own and other people's emotions. A person with high emotional intelligence has an increased ability to regulate emotions, to solve problems and to understand better the qualities that they need if they are to positively navigate the complexities of the social scene. Developing emotional intelligence, assertiveness, social skills and depth may not come particularly easy – but most things that are truly worthwhile in life are seldom easy!

Aristotle wisely pointed out that 'Anybody can become angry, that is easy; but to be angry with the right person, and to the right degree, and at the right time, for the right purpose, and in the right way, that is not within everybody's power and is not easy.' Hopefully this book will help parents and children to develop this perspicacity and that this will lead them to becoming more emotionally aware, more skilled socially and, ultimately, bully-proof.

Resources

The arts are very subjective so it is up to the parent or the teenager to have a look through these lists and take what they want and leave the rest. Although not all of these resources are about bullying, nevertheless they have been specially picked to develop tweens' and teenagers' emotional intelligence. The examples listed here are for both children and teenagers, but be sure to check the recommended age rating to decide what is appropriate for your child. You can enter a film, book, app or other website into the search bar at **www.commonsensemedia.org** to get an age rating and a detailed breakdown of any troubling content.

◼ Books

Bad Girls — Jacqueline Wilson

Blubber — Judy Blume

El Deafo – Cece Bell

Wonder – R. J. Palacio

Where the Red Fern Grows – Wilson Rawls

To Kill a Mockingbird — Harper Lee

The Diary of a Young Girl — Anne Frank

Carrie — Stephen King

Cat's Eye– Margaret Atwood

Of Mice and Men — John Steinbeck

The Fault in our Stars — John Green

The Alchemist — Paulo Coelho

Veronika Decides to Die — Paulo Coelho

The Catcher in the Rye — JD Salinger

Man's Search for Meaning — Viktor Frankl

So You've Been Publicly Shamed — Jon Ronson

Into the Wild — Jon Krakauer

The Bell Jar — Sylvia Plath

The Perks of Being a Wallflower — Stephen Chbosky

Odd Girl Out — Rachel Simmons

Nesthäkchen and the World War — Else Ury

The Beauty Myth — Naomi Wolf

Lord of the Flies — William Golding

Asking for It – Louise O'Neill

■ Music

'Hurt' — Johnny Cash

'Rise' — Public Image Limited

'Like a Rolling Stone' — Bob Dylan

'Positively Fourth Street' — Bob Dylan

'Trouble So Hard' — Moby

'Something Inside So Strong' — Labbi Siffre

'Don't Give Up' — Kate Bush & Peter Gabriel

'Tubthumping (I Get Knocked Down)' — Chumbawamba

'Everybody's Free (To Wear Sunscreen)' — Baz Luhrmann

'Mean' — Taylor Swift

'Heroes' — David Bowie

'I Saw It' — The Barenaked Ladies

'Jeremy' — Pearl Jam

'Creep' — Radiohead

'I Will Survive' — Gloria Gaynor

'Hold Your Own' — Kate Tempest

'Another Brick In The Wall' — Pink Floyd

'Everybody Hurts' — REM

'Not Afraid' — Eminem

'Ask' — The Smith

'At Seventeen' — Janis Ian

Films

Stand By Me

The Karate Kid

The Elephant Man

Carrie

Malcolm X

Amadeus

The Shawshank Redemption

Forrest Gump

Schindler's List

The King's Speech

Mean Girls

The Fat Boy Chronicles

Billy Elliot

Bully

Killing Us Softly

My Left Foot

Life is Beautiful

Empire of the Sun

Little Miss Sunshine

Bullied: A Student, a School and a Case That Made History

The Breakfast Club

Inside Out

Remember the Titans

The Pursuit of Happyness

Once Were Warriors

▨ Online Resources for Teenagers

www4.dcu.ie/abc/index.shtml The National Anti-Bullying Research & Resource Centre in DCU.

www.tacklebullying.ie Ireland's national anti-bullying website.

www.buddybench.ie Buddy Bench Ireland run emotional learning programmes in schools.

www.cybersafeireland.org An Irish website that empowers kids to be smart and safe online.

www.webwise.ie The Irish Internet Safety Awareness Centre provides support and information for parents and teachers.

www.belongto.org Supporting lesbian, gay, bisexual and transgender young people. See also their 'Stand Up: Don't Stand for Homophobic Bullying' campaign on YouTube.

www.getsafeonline.org Free expert online safety advice for parents and teenagers.

www.itgetsbetter.org Dan Savage's It Gets Better Project for LGBT youth.

www.bornthiswayfoundation.org The Born This Way Foundation was created by Lady Gaga to address mental health issues, empower youth and inspire bravery.

www.commonsensemedia.org/cyberbullying Common Sense Media's guide to cyberbullying.

www.facebook.com/stopbullyingspeakup Stop Bullying: Speak Up is Facebook's campaign against bullying.

www.athinline.org A Thin Line is MTV's campaign to stop digital abuse.

www.thetrevorproject.org The Trevor Project provides crisis intervention for lesbian, gay, bisexual, transgender and questioning youth.

www.bullybusters.org.uk Bully Busters is a step-by-step programme for reducing bullying based in the UK.

www.rootsofempathy.org Roots of Empathy is an international programme that brings babies into classroom to teach kids about development and empathy.

www.youthvoiceproject.com The Youth Voice Project asks students about their ideas for strategies against bullying and harassment in schools.

■ Parents' Guide to Social Media

Children should be 13 years old before they use social networking sites.

Keep mobile devices out of bedrooms.

Get into the habit of turning Wi-Fi off every night and always keep the password.

Put a password on the app store on your phone or tablet.

Use the mobile monitor 'Mobile Minder' or 'Selfie Cop' or check out other parental control apps.

Make sure settings are private and you know exactly who your children's friends and followers are.

Social media platforms can fall out of popularity quickly, so make sure you keep up to date with what your child is using.

It is illegal to procure or distribute indecent images of a person under 18.

www.connectsafely.org/pdfs/fbparents.pdf A parent's guide to Facebook.

www.connectafely.org/askfm-2/ A parent's guide to Ask FM.

www.connectsafely.org/wp-content/uploads/instagram_guide.pdf A parent's guide to Instagram.

www.connectsafely.org/a-parents-guide-to-snapchat/ A parent's guide to Snapchat.

www.net-aware.org.uk/networks/twitter A parent's guide to Twitter.

www.screentimelabs.com An app that gives parents control over time spent on tablets and smartphones

www.transl8it.com A website that translates text speak and internet slang

www.netlingo.com A website that helps parents penetrate social media chat lingo

www.commonsensemedia.org For age ratings, new media, apps and sites

www.safesearchkids.com A safe search engine with online guides for parents and teens

www.kidrex.org A child-friendly search engine

https://kids.youtube.com An app for YouTube users under the age of 13

www.google.ie/familysafety Advice on safe browsing for families

References

1. Oliver Holz and Fiona Shelton, *Education & Gender: Gender-specific education in different countries* (Münster: Waxmann Verlag, 2013), 32.

2. Holz and Shelton, *Education & Gender*.

3. *News at One*. RTÉ Radio One, 10 June 2016. Retrieved October 2016 http://www.rte.ie/radio1/news-at-one/programmes/2016/0610/794627-news-at-one-friday-10-june-2016/?clipid=2201094

4. Holz and Shelton, *Education & Gender*.

5. 'Bullying', Reachout.com. Last modified April 2017. Available at: http://ie.reachout.com/inform-yourself/bullying-and-personal-safety/bullying/

6. Julie Burchill, 'Meet the Cry-bully: a hideous hybrid of victim and victor'. *The Spectator*, 21 April 2015. Retrieved October 2016. Available at: https://blogs.spectator.co.uk/2015/04/meet-the-cry-bully-a-hideous-hybrid-of-victim-and-victor/

7. S. A. McLeod (2013). 'Erik Erikson'. Retrieved from www.simplypsychology.org/Erik-Erikson.html

8. Eileen Kennedy-Moore, 'Popular Kids': *Psychology Today*, 1 December 2013. Accessed October 2016. Available at: https://www.psychologytoday.com/blog/growing-friendships/201312/popular-kids

9. Kennedy-Moore, 'Popular Kids'.

10. Rachel Simmons, *Odd Girl Out* (London: Piatkus, 2012), xvii.

11. Martha Rosenberg, 'Author Brené Brown Discusses Embracing Our Ordinariness'. *Huffington Post*, 21 February 2011/Updated November 17, 2011. Retrieved October 2016. Available at: http://www.huffingtonpost.com/martha-rosenberg/embracing-our-ordinariness_b_802808.html

12. G. Gini, 'Social cognition and moral cognition in bullying: What's wrong?', *Aggressive Behavior* 32 (2006): 528–39; M. L. Obermann, 'Moral disengagement in self-reported and peer-nominated school bullying', *Aggressive Behavior* 37 (2011): 133–44; S. Perren, E. Gutzwiller-Helfenfinger, T. Malti and S. Hymel, 'Moral reasoning and emotion attributions of adolescent bullies, victims, and bully-victims', *British Journal of Developmental Psychology* 30 (2012): 511–30; T. Pozzoli, G. Gini and A. Vieno, 'Individual and class moral disengagement in bullying among elementary school children', *Aggressive Behavior* 38 (2012): 378–88.

13. G. Gini, T. Pozzoli and M. Hauser, 'Bullies have enhanced moral competence to judge relative to victims, but lack moral compassion', *Personality and Individual Differences* 50 (2011): 603–8.

14. R. J. R. Blair, 'The amygdala and ventromedial prefrontal cortex in morality and psychopathy', *Trends in Cognitive Sciences* 11 (2007): 387–92.

15. Rosalind Wiseman, *Queen Bees and Wannabes: Helping Your Daughter Survive Cliques, Gossip, Boyfriends, and Other Realities of Adolescence* (NY: Crown, 2002).

16. Joseph Stromberg, 'The neuroscientist who discovered he was a psychopath', *The Smithsonian*, 22 November 2013. Retrieved October 2016. Available at: http://www.smithsonianmag.com/science-nature/the-neuroscientist-who-discovered-he-was-a-psychopath-180947814/

17. Susan Donaldson James, 'Scientist Learns he has a psychopathic brain', *ABC News*, 30 November 2013. Retrieved October 2016. Available at: http://abcnews.go.com/Health/scientist-related-killers-learns-psychopaths-brain/story?id=21029246

18. 'Bullying', Reachout.com. Last modified April 2017. Available at: http://ie.reachout.com/inform-yourself/bullying-and-personal-safety/bullying/

19. Stephen King, *On Writing: A Memoir of the Craft.*

20. Russel Grieger, 'Happiness with others 4: Don't be needy', *Psychology Today* (2017): 28 February.

21. S. A. McLeod (2007). *The Milgram Experiment.* Retrieved from www.simplypsychology.org/milgram.html

22. Roy F. Baumeister, *Evil: Inside Human Violence and Cruelty* (NY: Holt Paperbacks, 1999), 2.

23. Laurent Bégue, Jean-Leon Beauvois, Didier Courbet, Dominique Oberle, Johan Lepage and Aaron A. Duke, 'Personality predicts obedience in a Milgram Paradigm', *Journal of Personality* 83 (2015): 299–306.

24. Cyberbullying Research Centre, 'Hannah Smith: Even More Tragic Than Originally Thought'. Accessed October 2016. Available at: http://cyberbullying.org/hannah-smith-even-more-tragic-than-originally-thought

25. Bronnie Ware, *The Top Five Regrets of the Dying* (Hay House, 2012), 82.

26. 'Five Things You Didn't Know About Bullying', PREVnet. Accessed October 2016. Available at: http://www.prevnet.ca/research/bullying-statistics/5-things-you-didnt-know-about-bullying

27. Richard Dahlstrom, *O2: Breathing New Life Into Faith* (OR: Harvest House, 2008), 63.

28. Snigdha Basu, '403 Vehicles, 45 People, Cops Ignored Dying Man. Driver Who Hit Him Finally Detained'. *NDTV*. Last modified August 2016. Available at: http://www.ndtv.com/delhi-news/everyone-ignored-dying-man-on-delhi-road-one-stole-his-mobile-phone-1442904

29. Lawrence Kohlberg, *The Development of Modes of Thinking and Choices in Years 10 to 16* (PhD Dissertation, University of Chicago, 1958).

30. Bibb Latané and John Darley, 'Bystander "Apathy"', *American Scientist*, 57 (1969): 244–68.

31. Cecilia Vega, 'Richmond rape witness describes the assault'. *ABC News*. 12 Nov 2009. Retrieved October 2016. Available at: http://abc7news.com/archive/7111732/

32. Latané and Darley, 'Bystander "Apathy"'.

33. Brenda Power, 'Turning a Blind Eye is a Crime', *Sunday Times*, 4 May 2014.

34. Barbara Coloroso, *The Bully, the Bullied, and the Bystander* (NY: HarperCollins, 2004).

35. Kathy Ann Murphy, 'Be the arrow, not the target', *Irish Independent*, 11 April 2012.

36. Emily Bazelon, *Sticks and Stones* (NY: Random House), 284.

37. Bazelon, *Sticks and Stones*, 266.

38. Jon Ronson, 'When online shaming goes too far', July 2015. Accessed October 2016. Available at: www.ted.com//talks/jon_ronson_what_happens_when_online_shaming_spirals_out_of_control/transcript

39. Ronson, 'When online shaming goes too far'.

40. Michele Borba, *UnSelfie: Why Empathetic Kids Succeed in Our All-About-Me World* (NY: Touchstone, 2016).

41. 'Ronan Hughes: Teen given 48 hours to pay £3k or private images would be sent to friends'. *Evening Herald*, 17 June 2015. Accessed October 2016. Available at: http://www.herald.ie/news/ronan-hughes-teen-given-48-hours-to-pay-3k-or-private-images-would-be-sent-to-friends-31308757.html

42. Jon Dean, 'Ronan Hughes: Teenager pleads "but I'm only 17" in text to blackmail gang before killing himself', *Daily Mirror*, 16 June 2015. Available at: http://www.mirror.co.uk/news/uk-news/ronan-hughes-teenager-pleads-but-5892900

43. 'Handbook for Safeguarding Sensitive Personally Identifiable Information', Homeland Security, March 2012. Available at: http://www.dhs.gov/xlibrary/assets/privacy/privacy_guide_spii_handbook.pdf

44. 'The CyberSafe Ireland Family Agreement', CyberSafe Ireland. Accessed October 2016. Available at: http://cybersafeireland.org/index.php/the-cybersafeireland-family-agreement/

45. 'Girls and their Frenemies', SMC Education Blog, September 2016. Accessed October 2016. Available at: http://smceducationblog.tumblr.com/post/150629869120/girls-and-their-frenemies

46. Andrew Solomon, 'How the worst moments in our lives make us who we are', May 2014. Accessed October 2016. Available at: http://www.ted.com/talks/andrew_solomon_how_the_worst_moments_in_our_lives_make_us_who_we_are/transcript?language=en

47. Vitelli, R., PhD, 'What makes anti-bullying programmes effective?' *Psychology Today*, January 27th 2016 https://www.psychologytoday.com/blog/media-spotlight/20101/what-makes-anti-bullying-programs-effective

48. T. J. McIntyre, 'Sexting and the law in Ireland', January 2010. Available at: http://www.tjmcintyre.com/2010/01/sexting-and-law-in-ireland.html

49. Preston Ni, 'How to increase your emotional intelligence', *Psychology Today*, 5 October 2014. Accessed October 2016. Available at: https://www.psychologytoday.com/blog/communication-success/201410/how-increase-your-emotional-intelligence-6-essentials

50. Andrew Solomon, 'How the worst moments in our lives make us who we are'.

51. David Coleman, 'Why I'm in favour of kids fighting back against the schoolyard bully', *Irish Independent*, 3 March 2016. Accessed October 2016. Available at: http://www.independent.ie/life/family/family-features/david-coleman-why-im-in-favour-of-kids-fighting-back-against-the-schoolyard-bully-34505548.html

52. *Miriam O'Callaghan Show*, RTÉ 1, 26 June 2016.

53. Ellie Austin, 'Who can we turn to now?' *The Sunday Times Magazine*, February 26, 2017.

54. Rachael Bletchly, '"I grew up feeling ugly, awkward and horrible": Christina Hendricks on her emergence as a sex icon.' *The Mirror*, 17 February 2012.

55. Kenneth Ginsburg, *Building Resilience in Children and Teens* (IL: American Academy of Pediatrics, 2011).

56. Bazelon, *Sticks and Stones*, 298–9.

57. Carol Dweck, *Mindset: The New Psychology of Success* (NY: Random House, 2006).

58. Alice Munroe, *Open Secrets* (NY: Random House, 1995).

59. Bazelon, *Sticks and Stones*, 305.

60. Bazelon, *Sticks and Stones*, 306.